ONE FOR THE AGES

ONE FOR THE AGES

JACK NICKLAUS AND THE 1986 MASTERS

TOM CLAVIN

CHICAGO
REVIEW
PRESS

Library of Congress Cataloging-in-Publication Data

Clavin, Thomas

  One for the Ages : Jack Nicklaus and the 1986 Masters / Tom Clavin.

    p. cm.

  Includes bibliographical references and index.

  ISBN 978-1-56976-705-4 (hardcover)

  1. Masters Golf Tournament (1986) 2. Masters Golf Tournament—History.
3. Golf—United States—History. 4. Nicklaus, Jack. 5. Golfers—United States.
I. Title.

GV970.3.M37C57 2011

796.352092—dc22

[B]

2010034924

Grateful acknowledgment is made to the estate of Herbert Warren Wind for permission to reprint excerpts from "Nicklaus: All the Way Back," by Herbert Warren Wind, originally published in the June 2, 1986, issue of the *New Yorker*, and to Simon & Schuster for extracts reprinted with the permission of Simon & Schuster, Inc., from *Jack Nicklaus: My Story* by Jack Nicklaus with Ken Bowden. Copyright © 1997 by Jack Nicklaus. All rights reserved.

Interior design: Jonathan Hahn

© 2011 by Tom Clavin

All rights reserved

Published by Chicago Review Press, Incorporated

814 North Franklin Street

Chicago, Illinois 60610

ISBN 978-1-56976-705-4

Printed in the United States of America

5 4 3 2 1

To my mother, Gertrude (O'Brien) Clavin—my first patron.

ALTHOUGH THE LAST, NOT LEAST.
—*King Lear*, Act I, Scene I

CONTENTS

AUTHOR'S NOTE

I was tempted in this book to focus exclusively on the four days and seventy-two holes of the 1986 Masters golf tournament. The event was a milestone in Masters history because it reflected more than ever before how truly international professional golf had become. It also reflected much of the history of golf in the United States, with participants ranging from promising twentysomething amateurs to retired legends such as Gene Sarazen and Sam Snead. And it was quite simply one of the most dramatic major championships ever held, a Masters that will never be forgotten.

But I chose to expand the scope of the book, for two reasons. The first is that the story of the Masters is intertwined with the story of golf's greatest player, Jack Nicklaus. Of the many events he won around the world from the 1950s into the 1990s, he is associated most with the one held every April at the Augusta National Golf Club. *One for the Ages* is intended to acquaint readers with much of the action and many of the personalities that led to that pivotal 1986 event when golf's finest player had his finest hour.

The second reason is that the action didn't really heat up until the third day, Saturday. Over the first couple days, even seasoned sports reporters chose not to cover each hole in detail; in an age before the Internet, writers worked up emerging themes and angles for feature stories rather than tweeting or blogging about every unremarkable shot as the media do today. Also, today we are accustomed to almost wall-to-wall television coverage by CBS. In 1986, however, such coverage was limited Thursday through Saturday, and even on Sunday it didn't begin until the final group had already played several holes. As a result, this book's treatment of the first thirty-six holes of the 1986 Masters is not as detailed as would be the case if this year's Masters were to be written about twenty-five years from now.

It is my hope that when you finish this book you will feel some of the thrill that the patrons of Augusta felt in April 1986 and will have a good understanding of and appreciation for a very special sporting event that has captivated generations of players as well as fans.

ACKNOWLEDGMENTS

I am grateful to those people whose memories of and insights about the 1986 Masters Tournament were so helpful, especially Tom Watson, Mark McCumber, Pat Summerall, Verne Lundquist, Tom Kite, and Raymond Floyd. Others whose recollections were useful include Seve Ballesteros, Ben Crenshaw, Bernhard Langer, Jim Nantz, Arnold Palmer, and Lee Trevino.

David Owen's *The Making of the Masters* was a particularly good resource. It offers a vivid portrait of Clifford Roberts, is filled with facts, and is just a darn good read. I thank him for writing such a fine book.

Among those who were helpful to me in various ways during the writing of this book were Steve Auch at the Jack Nicklaus Museum, Bob Bubka, Judge Edward Burke Sr., Nicole Ciaramella at the U.S. Golf Association, Bob Drury and Denise McDonald, Steve Ethun at the Augusta National Golf Club, Michael and Shelly Gambino, Michael Griffith and Nancy Grigor, Valerie Hanley, Phil Keith, Ann Liguori, Amanda Jones and Sean Moores at the *Augusta Chronicle*, Colin Murray at the PGA Tour, Danny Peary and Suzanne Rafer, Tina Piette, Lynne Scanlon, Val and Min-Myn Schaffner, Bill Scheft, Nat Sobel, Scott Tolley at the Nicklaus Companies, and the staff at the East Hampton Library.

Gratitude goes to my editors, Yuval Taylor and Lisa Reardon, and Mary Kravenas and others at Chicago Review Press, and to Scott Gould, Bob Rosen, and Craig Foster at RLR Associates.

My final thanks go to my children, Brendan Clavin and Kathryn Clavin, and to Leslie Reingold, who hung in there despite all the bogeys.

ONE FOR THE AGES

THE FIRST ROUND

THURSDAY, APRIL 10

1

If Jack Nicklaus didn't feel the weight of age on his shoulders when he woke up that morning, he might have during the official starter ceremony to begin the 1986 Masters, the fiftieth in the tournament's history. The starters were two older legends, Gene Sarazen and Sam Snead, who represented the first two great generations of American players. Well over a decade ago, Nicklaus had surpassed both of them in majors championships won—in fact, he had collected more majors than Sarazen and Snead combined.

The tradition of honorary starters opening the Masters began with Jock Hutchison and Fred McLeod, who won the first two PGA Seniors Championships in 1937 and 1938, respectively. Fittingly, these two gentlemen hit the first ceremonial tee shots at the Masters in 1963, when Nicklaus won his first green jacket. Hutchison continued the honors through 1973, and McLeod's final appearance was in 1976. After a gap of a few years, Byron Nelson and Sarazen revived the tradition in 1981. For just one year, in 1983, Ken Venturi was a ceremonial starter—an odd pick, given that he had not won a Masters and was only fifty-one at the time. The following year Snead signed on as the third ceremonial starter with Nelson and Sarazen. For the 1986 Masters, the seventy-four-year-old Nelson was unable to participate, leaving the now-traditional task to Sarazen and Snead. The man known as the Squire was wearing, as he always did on the golf course, knickers (this time cream-colored ones), and the dapper Snead, who during his career had been dubbed the Slammer, was wearing a red sweater and his signature straw hat.

Sarazen had been born in 1902. That was the same year as Bobby Jones, whose influence was still deeply felt at Augusta National even fifteen years after his death. Sarazen and Jones and Walter Hagen—almost ten years older, but he kept winning into his forties—had been the players to beat in their various tournaments, beginning when Sir Walter won his first U.S. Open in 1914. They had dueled each other in U.S. Opens and British Opens and in tense exhibition matches over the years, with Sarazen the last one of the three to capture one of the Opens, the British in 1932. With the fast pace of U.S. sports, this was ancient history by the mid-1980s. Yet here was the Squire, a pugnacious five foot five, about to strike his ball on the first tee fifty-one years after his first Masters.

Snead, along with Nelson and Ben Hogan—all born in 1912—had been the next generation of players to beat beginning in the late 1930s. It was hard, however, to view Snead as ancient history, even though he was a month shy of turning seventy-four years old. First of all, the Slammer looked great, and he still had the sweetest swing in golf. The face under the familiar hat was lined and weathered, but the eyes twinkled, and his language still had more salt in it than a bag of Georgia peanuts. Snead had played in the Masters until only three years previous and had long been a force at Augusta National. In 1963 it was Snead himself, then fifty-one, whom the twenty-three-year-old Nicklaus had had to battle down the stretch to win his first Masters. Snead was no lingering figure from the distant past. Instead, he was anticipating a perfect first-hole drive into the cool southwesterly breeze to warm the crowd at Augusta National.

If anything, it was not Snead but Jack Nicklaus whom many of the other players, reporters, broadcasters, and even a few Augusta National members considered to be a figure from an earlier time—maybe not the distant past but almost certainly the past. Even he had said, "After 1980, I was no longer the man to beat" on the Professional Golfers' Association (PGA) Tour, and that turned out to include the majors. He had not won an official tournament of any kind in two years, and twenty majors had come and gone without him claiming victory.

To Nicklaus, the number of worldwide wins was a good yardstick of career achievement, and he had ninety-eight, with seventy-three of them on the PGA Tour. But it was victories in majors that defined greatness; Jack had nineteen—two U.S. Amateur Championships, five Masters titles, five PGA Championships, four U.S. Opens, and three British Opens. Jack had turned forty-six in January 1986 and had been competing professionally for twenty-four years. Along with Arnold Palmer and Gary Player, he was a member of the third great triumvirate. That group's origins lay almost three decades in the past.

His last victory in a major had been in 1980. It was a thrilling one, the PGA Championship at Oak Hill in Rochester, the city that had produced Walter Hagen, who remained second on the list of number of professional majors won with eleven, despite almost half a century passing since his retirement. The PGA triumph had come only two months after Nicklaus won his eighteenth major, the U.S. Open at Baltusrol in New Jersey, when his 63 in the first round had tied the Open record set by Johnny Miller in 1973.

But the intervening years had seen one frustration after another in the majors, and every year began with another birthday. The year before, in 1985, it had seemed like little was left in the tank. His sixth-place finish at Augusta offered a glimmer of hope, especially his final-round 69. But at Oakland Hills in Michigan, where the ghost of Hagen truly lingered—he had been the club's first head pro—Nicklaus opened with a 76-73 and missed the U.S. Open cut. No happiness was to be found at Royal St. George's in England: he missed another British Open cut with rounds of 77 and 75. A tie for thirty-second in the PGA Championship at Cherry Hills in Colorado hardly revived his career. How ironic that it was at Cherry Hills that Nicklaus had first attracted widespread attention a quarter century ago, when as an amateur he had battled Ben Hogan and the eventual winner, Arnold Palmer, for the 1960 U.S. Open.

As the starter ceremony got under way, Sarazen was introduced; clearly, he enjoyed the applause. Ringing the tee box were reporters and photographers, wide-eyed spectators, several players, and members of the Tournament Committee (all in green jackets), including its chairman, Hord Hardin. The seventy-four-year-old, who revered the Masters traditions, had in 1980 become only the third chairman in the event's history.

The Squire blew on his hands, addressed the ball with his driver, and swung. The ball flew off to the left. There was a brief, awkward pause, and then Sarazen was allowed a mulligan. His next drive brought smiles to every face—the ball split the fairway. Even more generous applause followed.

Though not a vain man, Nicklaus had to wonder if he would ever again hear applause like what he had received while walking up the eighteenth fairway at Baltusrol in 1980. His previous U.S. Open title had been eight years earlier, at Pebble Beach, and because he was forty in 1980, not many people had given him a chance. But he had bookended that first-round 63 with a final-round 68 to win his fourth Open by two strokes over Isao Aoki, the best of a crop of good golfers Japan was exporting. Nicklaus locked up the tournament by sinking a birdie putt of twenty-two feet on 17. His 272 total had dashed the Open scoring record. "Jack is back! Jack is back!" the crowd had chanted, and it was posted on the scoreboard, too. He told them, "You'll never know how sweet it is." The PGA Championship had been icing on the cake—and his swan song, many now believed.

And then, as far as majors were concerned, Jack was indeed history. In his preview of the 1986 Masters in that past Sunday's sports section of the *Atlanta Journal-Constitution*, Tom McCollister had flatly declared, "Nicklaus is gone, done. He just doesn't have the game anymore. It's rusted from lack of use." He further emphasized, "He's 46, and nobody that old wins the Masters." When Jack and Barbara Nicklaus arrived at the house they rented for the week near Augusta National, the couple found that a friend of theirs, Tom Montgomery, had taped McCollister's article to the refrigerator door to tease Jack, or perhaps light a fire under him. Jack left it there.

McCollister was right about advanced age and the Masters. When Gary Player won his third green jacket in 1978, he was forty-two, and that was considered pretty grizzled. (The oldest man to win *any* major was Julius Boros, who won the PGA Championship at forty-eight in 1968. No one near that age had come close in a major since, and an asterisk on Boros's achievement is that the PGA event did not have the same stature as the three other major championships.) Here, in 1986, Jack was already four years older than the fitness fanatic Player had been, and some golf writers had tactfully pointed out that he was "paunchier" than before.

Arnold Palmer, who had played in his first Masters in 1955, had spoken jokingly about Nicklaus to a reporter at Augusta National. He recalled how Jack had once vowed to him that he would no longer be out there competing on golf courses and certainly not in the Masters at forty, and sure as heck not at forty-five. Arnold told the reporter he had responded, "Well, Jack, I hope you still come to Augusta so you can watch me play." When asked if at fifty-six he still could win a major, Arnold, always confident and still swaggering, replied, "Sure. You just need everything to go right just that one weekend."

Now it was Snead's turn to tee off. He too blew on his hands, then made the familiar sweet swing. When he was in his prime, the Slammer's swing had been admired and envied by every golfer. He didn't disappoint this morning; his ball bounced down the fairway past Sarazen's.

Eighty-eight players—ten of them amateurs—were waiting, and now the fiftieth Masters Tournament could begin. It had come a long way in a half century from truly humble beginnings, and some must have wondered if anything in its present or future could compete with the many thrills for which the Masters was already known.

2

Few sports champions were as revered as Robert Tyre "Bobby" Jones Jr., born in Atlanta on March 17, 1902. Jones suffered from various ailments as a young boy, for which learning and playing golf were prescribed. He was coached by Stewart Maiden, a Scottish club professional, at the East Lake Golf Club in Atlanta. He was also schooled by his father, Colonel Robert P. Jones, who was himself a very good player.

Robert Jr. won his first children's tournament at age six. He began to receive national attention at fourteen when he lasted into the third round of the U.S. Amateur Championship. At that same age he won the Georgia Amateur Championship, and the next year, 1917, he won the Southern Amateur for the first time (he would win the event again in 1920 and 1922). After touring the United States with Alexa Stirling and others to do exhibition matches as Red Cross and other war-relief fundraisers during World War I, Jones took a step onto the international stage by being on the American team that defeated Canada in matches in 1919 and 1920. He tied for second in the 1919 Canadian Open. He was eighteen when he qualified for the U.S. Open in 1920, and for the first two rounds he was paired with Harry Vardon, from the island of Jersey, who had six British Open victories and had won the U.S. Open in 1900. Jones was also on the U.S. team at the inaugural Walker Cup

Match in 1922; the Americans defeated the British squad at National Golf Links in Southampton, New York. (To this day, that first Walker Cup Match remains the only major international event ever played at what is still judged annually as one of the best courses in the United States.)

Certainly, winning helped to elevate Jones to heroic status. At age twenty-one, at the Inwood Country Club in Inwood, New York, he won his first U.S. Open. He won his second Open in 1926 at the Scioto Country Club in Columbus, Ohio—witnessed by thirteen-year-old Charles Nicklaus, Jack's father. He won a third Open in a playoff in 1929, and as part of what came to be known as the Grand Slam, he captured his fourth Open in 1930. It would be twenty-three years before another player won four Opens: Ben Hogan.

Jones also won three British Opens and was especially admired at the "home of golf," St. Andrews, where he won his second Claret Jug in 1927. As an amateur he was not eligible for the PGA Championship, but he won five U.S. Amateur Championships and a British Amateur, considered majors at the time. He won thirteen of the twenty major tournaments he entered, a career winning percentage that has never been duplicated. Even more remarkable, of the last twelve Open championships he played—nine U.S. Opens and three British Opens—he finished first or second in eleven of them. And, of course, he was four-for-four in 1930, earning the so-called Grand Slam. Twice he was given ticker-tape parades in New York City.

Yet more than championships awed the public. Jones steadfastly clung to his amateur status throughout the 1920s, and that was seen as virtuous. During the same decade, Walter Hagen earned four British Opens and five PGA Championships to go with U.S. Open victories in 1914 and 1919; the flamboyant "Haig" was popular among most golf fans, but as a professional who played for money, he wasn't given the reverence Jones was. Jones's stature was also enhanced by his reputation for honesty and loyalty to his wife and family—especially when he was compared with the hard-partying, skirt-chasing Hagen. Being a handsome man who looked quite the boyish gentleman in news photographs was an advantage too.

After the Grand Slam, at only twenty-eight, exhausted by the strain and attention of his achievement, Jones retired to Atlanta to attend to his family and his law practice. The departure was enormously disappointing to sports fans. When it was announced three years later that he would play competitively again in a tournament at a golf course he and a partner were building in Augusta, Georgia, that was cause for rejoicing.

The partner was Clifford Roberts. He had been born in 1894 on a farm in Iowa, and his full name was actually the much stuffier Charles DeClifford Roberts Jr. His parents had five children, which was an achievement considering that his father was almost always on the road chasing numerous projects that would make the family rich. He never found the right one.

Unlike Bobby Jones, who would always call Georgia home, Roberts had an itinerant childhood, with the Roberts family moving around to follow the father's next financial expedition. When Clifford was nineteen and the family was living in Texas, his mother committed suicide with a shotgun. After his father remarried a much younger woman, Clifford decided it was time to hit the road himself—as a traveling salesman. Then in 1917 he went to seek his fortune in New York City. He didn't find it but instead found himself broke. It was probably a blessing that he was drafted into the army. He was in France for only a month when World War I ended in November 1918. When he was back in the States the following year, Roberts took another shot at New York. This time he stayed, working in the stock market. He became a fairly successful businessman during the Roaring Twenties. He stayed in the business even after significant losses in the 1929 stock market crash and during the next few years after that.

Roberts had taken up golf in the 1920s and was a member of the Knollwood Country Club in Westchester County. He first met Bobby Jones when the latter played an exhibition match there in 1925. The following year the U.S. Amateur Championship was held at the Baltusrol course in New Jersey, and Roberts was there for the final match, in which George Von Elm beat Jones 2 and 1. Roberts was among several men who joined Jones for a consolation drink. A good friendship was formed, and Roberts and Jones kept in touch in the ensuing years.

During the coldest months in New York, Roberts took trips to Augusta, Georgia, to play golf. In the winter of 1929–30, he and Jones were both vacationing at the Bon Air–Vanderbilt Hotel, and it is likely there that they first discussed building a course in Augusta. The discussions between the two men became more serious after Jones earned the Grand Slam and the celebrity that went with it. He believed that a golf course elsewhere than Atlanta would give him and his family some privacy while he played golf only for enjoyment and male camaraderie.

Jones could be viewed as the captain of Augusta National, the public face of the place, but Roberts was the executive officer who got things done, the hands-on nuts-and-bolts guy. He was one of a group—also consisting of Jones, Bob Jones Sr., and three businessmen—that became the Fruitland Manor Corporation. In 1931 the corporation bought 365 acres for fifteen thousand dollars and the assumption of the previous owner's sixty-thousand-dollar debt to the Georgia Railroad Bank. About half of the land was leased to what would become the Augusta National Golf Club. On the property was Magnolia Avenue (later Lane), so named because of the trees that lined it, the seeds of which were first planted in 1859 or 1860. The property also contained a plantation house built in 1854.

The original plan was for something much more ambitious than a simple golf course. Jones and Roberts wanted to tear down the plantation house and replace it with a modern structure for a clubhouse. There would be two courses, the second one for women. There would also be tennis and squash courts, a bridle path, and houses that members could purchase or rent. All this would be underwritten by memberships the corporation sold for $350 each and annual dues of $60. Jones and Roberts estimated that they could persuade eighteen hundred people to join, and that would provide more than enough capital.

They hired the golf architect Alister MacKenzie—who had created Cypress Point next to Pebble Beach in California—to design the Augusta National Golf Club. But Roberts would oversee every aspect of construction and communicate Jones's ideas about the course's features to MacKenzie.

By February 1932 the design was mostly completed, and construction began. Laborers were glad to have jobs, and they worked furiously. Jones was able to play his first round on the course that August, and he liked what he saw. Perhaps, as he and Roberts had envisioned, Augusta National could be the finest golf course in America.

However, it was not the best of ideas to have lofty ambitions for a great golf course in the early years of the Depression. Roberts and Jones didn't come within a 3-wood of their membership goal.

Today, an available membership at Augusta National is more rare than a hole-in-one. In 1932, with the country swallowed by the Depression, even the fame of Bobby Jones couldn't fill the membership roll. Many bills went unpaid, though Roberts managed to pay the workers so that the course would be completed. Poor MacKenzie, who today is credited with designing one of the best courses in the world, received only two thousand of his originally requested ten-thousand-dollar fee. He last saw Augusta National the same month that Jones played his first round, and he died almost broke in January 1934, before the first tournament was played there.

Augusta National officially opened a year earlier, in January 1933. A contingent of New York businessmen led by eminent sportswriter and Jones's friend Grantland Rice took a train down for several days of wining and dining and rounds of golf with Jones and Francis Ouimet. (Ouimet was also a lifelong amateur and the hero of the 1913 U.S. Open at the Country Club in Massachusetts, where the twenty-one-year-old defeated Harry Vardon and Ted Ray in a playoff.) Jones and Roberts hoped that the party atmosphere and freshly built beauty of the golf course would translate into multiple memberships. However, bad weather made for a rather dismal outing, and visitors left without the hoped-for optimistic impression of Augusta in winter. The club continued to struggle financially, with most of the burden to keep it open falling on Roberts's shoulders.

In February 1933, Prescott Bush, the father of one future U.S. president, the grandfather of another, and a prominent member of the U.S. Golf Association, played at Augusta National. Apparently, his experience was positive enough that he floated the idea of the U.S. Open being held there in 1934. The USGA eventually rejected the idea because it didn't want to move the Open from June, the best time for a golf tournament in the Northeast and Midwest, to March or April, the best time in Georgia, but the thought of having a high-profile tournament there stuck. Roberts arranged for the PGA of America to include one event at Augusta National in its 1934 schedule. It was to be called the Augusta National Invitation Tournament. Surely, this would put the course on the American golf map and attract members to the club.

The trump card, of course, was Bobby Jones. His participation would be the only way to attract name players and paying spectators (at $2.20 a ticket). But Jones was hesitant about playing, because he had not been in a competition since 1930. He had to be too rusty to successfully take on the country's best players. His nature dictated that he could think only of winning, and performing poorly on his own course would be embarrassing. Without him, however, Augusta National would lose money hosting the tournament, so Jones had little choice but to participate.

Many of the top golfers arrived in Augusta the third week of March 1934 to play alongside Jones. (Exceptions were Joe Kirkwood and Gene Sarazen, who couldn't pass up the revenue from an exhibition tour of South America.) Jones, having managed to squeeze in a few practice rounds, shot 76-74-72-72 and tied for thirteenth with reigning British Open champion Denny Shute and his old archrival, Walter Hagen.

The first champion of an official tournament at Augusta National was crowned on March 25, when Horton Smith carded a seventy-two-hole total of 284. He collected fifteen hundred dollars for his steady play. By far the most popular victory would have been by Jones, but the fact that he had played at all immediately gave the invitational at Augusta National a distinction no other tournament in the world could claim.

If there was any player to truly feel sorry for, it was Billy Burke. He had been invited to Augusta because of his win three years earlier at the U.S. Open. It had been a marathon event at the Inverness Club in Toledo, Ohio, over the July 4 weekend. After the final two rounds, played on Independence Day itself, Burke and George Von Elm were tied at 292. The USGA rules at the time required a thirty-six-hole playoff the next day. At the end of it, both players had shot 149 and were still tied. Out they went the next day in the midsummer steam bath to stagger through another thirty-six holes. Von Elm was in the lead by a stroke after eighteen holes, but on the second eighteen Burke shot 71 to his rival's 73 and became the National champion, earning the crown that had been vacated by Bobby Jones.

He must have used up all his luck in 1931, because the final three holes at the 1934 Invitational were torture for Burke as he tried to catch Smith. As the *New York Times* reported in its March 26 issue, on the last three holes Burke's putts hung so close to the lip of the cup that the crowd each time yelled for him to wait for a breeze to blow the ball in. "Each time the ball seemed to be looking down into the cup. A wind was blowing, but it never seemed to strike the ball." Burke had to tap each one in. The *Times* account concluded, "If just two of them had dropped, he would have had a tie, had three of them fallen, he would have been the winner. But that is golf."

3

Magnolia Lane, the main entrance to Augusta National, runs 330 yards from Washington Road to the circle before the clubhouse. The five dozen magnolias that line the lane are usually not yet in bloom the second week in April, but the branches that meet over the entranceway offer a canopy of green leaves.

The clubhouse is the same structure that sat on the property when the consortium led by Jones and Roberts bought it in 1931, and a few intimations remain of the 1854 farmhouse it once was. A longtime Masters reporter for the *Charlotte Observer*, Ron Green Sr., described the clubhouse as "something out of *Gone with the Wind*. White, three floors, porches, a cupola, shaded by big trees, two chimneys, a sweeping view of the golf course spilling away downhill toward Rae's Creek. Breakfast favorites: country ham and grits with redeye gravy," usually in the Trophy Room where the members eat. "Dessert of choice: peach cobbler."

The article described trophy cases bathed in soft light; decades-old golf clubs on display; portraits of Masters chairmen and players, with Bobby Jones prominently featured; muted colors; simple wood furniture; and a casual atmosphere. "Quiet elegance" is the phrase Green used. Within the clubhouse is the Crow's Nest, a twelve-hundred-square-foot suite that can house up to five amateur players.

When the Masters week of 1986 began, Augusta National was immaculate, and not just because this was the fiftieth Masters, the event's golden anniversary. The course was always in immaculate shape the second week in April. The fairways had been overseeded with fifty thousand pounds of rye grass to produce the particular green that Roberts had demanded. They had been mowed and the putting surfaces trimmed to within a whisker of perfection. The white-brown sand in the bunkers was as smooth as the beaches of an undiscovered Pacific island. Hundreds of dogwoods exploded with white and pink petals. The lakes had been dyed blue, and even the food wrappers, cups, utensils, and napkins were green so that no litter would be discerned by the television audience.

And, of course, there were the azaleas. More than thirty varieties thrive at Augusta National. Television cameras love to pan them when the CBS broadcast is about to go to or is coming back from commercial breaks. They are in full bloom during Masters week, bursting with white and purple flowers, and they are complemented by dozens of strains of ornamental shrubs, not to mention the dogwoods.

"The golf course has never been better," observed Tom Watson after a midweek practice round. "It's playing a little longer because there's more grass on the fairways, but they're excellent. The greens are firmer than they've been for a long time, which I like. It's going to be the same as it's always been here—the best iron player and the best putter will win."

The Masters is the youngest of the four majors and the only one played on the same course every year, a distinction that has added to its mystique. That, its association with Bobby Jones, and its many quaint and respected traditions make the tournament one that every player wants to win. Champions are welcomed "home" to Augusta National every year and are able to continue playing in the tournament. With the other three majors, once a champion's exemption expires, he has to earn his way back in. The Masters is also the first major championship tournament of the year, eight months after the last, and thus is especially challenging.

"To many golfers, Augusta National indeed is the Mt. Everest of the game," wrote Dave Anderson in his April 11, 1986, column in the *New York Times*.

Besides the Masters, the closest a major has come to being played on the same course has been the British Open (founded in 1860), which adheres to a rotation of familiar courses. Courses were inserted and removed over the decades, but the top golfers in the world could expect to compete for the Claret Jug on certain courses every summer—among them Carnoustie, Muirfield, Royal Birkdale, St. Andrews, and Turnberry.

Next came the U.S. Open. Since 1895, several golf clubs have hosted the Open four or more times: Baltusrol, Inverness, Merion, Myopia, Oakland Hills, Oakmont, Olympic, Pebble Beach, Shinnecock Hills, and Winged Foot. More than forty Opens have been hosted by only ten clubs. But they have been spread out over 115 years: the host course each year has been different from the year before; if a repeat course, it has undergone significant changes since it last hosted; and the courses are in different parts of the country. For example, in 2009 the Open was held at Bethpage Black on Long Island, New York, the next year it was at Pebble Beach in California, in 2011 it is at the Congressional Country Club in Maryland, and in 2012 it will be back out on the West Coast, at the Olympic Club in San Francisco.

The PGA Championship has been all over the place. Like the U.S. Open, in its early years the event was most often held in the Northeast, because that was where the PGA of America was originally headquartered and where the majority of the golf population lived. Eighteen PGA Championships have shared sites that held Opens, but in recent decades the PGA has gone farther afield to hold its championship, including such courses as Crooked Stick in Indiana, Laurel Valley in Pennsylvania, Sahalee in Washington State, and Whistling Straits in Wisconsin. In 2012 it will take place at Kiawah Island in South Carolina, where the "War by the Shore" Ryder Cup Match was held in 1991.

Since the Masters has a permanent home at Augusta National, some players and golf writers have contended that the tournament is not the strongest major. Because of the familiarity of the setting, they say, the more experienced players have the advantage of calling on their memory banks to play certain shots and avoid or at least get out of trouble year after year. (Another argument is that the high number of amateurs invited and the ongoing participation of past champions in their fifties or older result in a weaker field.) That could explain Nicklaus's five green jackets and Palmer's four, though it does not then explain Harry Vardon's six British Open victories, the four U.S. Opens each by Nicklaus, Willie Anderson, Bobby Jones, and Ben Hogan, and the five PGA Championships each won by Nicklaus and Hagen, all majors that lack a permanent home.

Also because of the tournament's permanence, Augusta National has continued to be a work in progress. Significant changes have been made every year to prepare for the Masters, and many of the changes made since Nicklaus's first victory there in 1963 have lengthened the course. But even before Nicklaus first drove down Magnolia Lane, Roberts and Jones and their successors had always been trying to improve the quality and challenge of Augusta National. From the first tournament in 1934 through 1986, play was affected by at least seventy significant alterations to the course.

The very first one that made a big difference was that after the inaugural event, the front side became the back side—in other words, the first nine holes became the second nine holes, and vice versa. In the 1935 Masters, players teed off from what had been the tenth hole. As radical a change as that was, it was only the beginning, as Roberts was always looking for ways to make Augusta National more attractive and challenging.

By the 1986 Masters week, Augusta National had grown to just under seven thousand yards in length. It had bent grass, after a switch from Bermuda grass in 1980. Each of the eighteen holes had its own name:

1 Tea Olive (par 4)
2 Pink Dogwood (par 5)
3 Flowering Peach (par 4)
4 Flowering Crab Apple (par 3)
5 Magnolia (par 4)
6 Juniper (par 3)
7 Pampas (par 4)
8 Yellow Jasmine (par 5)
9 Carolina Cherry (par 4)
10 Camellia (par 4)
11 White Dogwood (par 4)

12 Golden Bell (par 3)
13 Azalea (par 5)
14 Chinese Fir (par 4)
15 Firethorn (par 5)
16 Redbud (par 3)
17 Nandina (par 4)
18 Holly (par 4)

The most famous section of the golf course is holes 11 through 13. They are found in the southeast section of the course, near Rae's Creek and one of its tributaries. Many a Masters was won or lost there depending on a player's ability to stay out of the water. In his coverage of the 1958 Masters for *Sports Illustrated*, Herbert Warren Wind first referred to this trio of holes as Amen Corner, harking back to a jazz recording, "Shouting at Amen Corner," that he remembered hearing while a college student. It was well known that more than once Nicklaus had called the 155-yard twelfth hole the most demanding in the world, and many a tournament leader— including Nicklaus, in 1981—has been led to ruin by putting his tee shot into Rae's Creek.

On the Sunday before the fiftieth Masters, the population of Augusta swelled as it has for decades, with spectators arriving along with the first wave of players, many of them with their families. A few optimistic fans showed up hoping to scalp badges, and a few succeeded. Other than that, there were no badges to be bought. The credentials needed to gain entrance to Augusta National stopped being sold long before 1986—they began selling out in 1966—and the ones in existence were passed down from one family member to another. It was probably easier in 1986 to get into the Kremlin than into Augusta National without a badge.

Some of the players were ready for practice rounds on Monday. It depended on who had been where the previous week. Some players had competed in the Greensboro Open that week, either because they saw it as a good tune-up for the Masters or because they simply needed the paycheck. Unless they didn't make the cut, these players spent Sunday night and Monday in transit. Others preferred to follow their own practice routine and leave a little early for Augusta. But Tuesday would be the first day when everyone would be playing practice rounds.

The weather, often lovely in Augusta in April, was anything but benign that Tuesday. It rained heavily, with a hailstorm for dramatic effect. Practice rounds were hampered, and thus the most important event of that day, the Champions Dinner, was especially welcome. The Champions Dinner is one of the more popular Masters traditions. The previous year's champion presides over the event, and has the privilege of choosing the dishes that will be served to the past champions in attendance. The flow of wine and anecdotes makes for a convivial time. Ben Hogan first came up with the idea in 1952, when he was the reigning champion after his final-round 68 had earned him his long-sought first green jacket in 1951.

Wednesday was the first of a series of sunny and dry days that would become warmer as the breeze softened. Players became more serious as they fine-tuned their game with the intention of getting off to a good start in the first round on Thursday. There was a full complement of practice rounds on the course, while others were doggedly determined to get most of their work done on the driving ranges. At Augusta National there were two ranges, on the east and west sides of Magnolia Lane. The east-side range is closer to Washington Road, and over the years, as the players grew bigger and stronger and hit longer drives, balls began hitting cars driving on it. As a result, four years earlier the west range had been enlarged, and players were directed there for their annual pre-tournament range work. Additionally, an eleven-foot-high net was placed 245 yards from the teeing area, and 15 yards beyond that was another net, this one twenty-three feet high.

Sam Snead was out on the west range, though not necessarily to prepare for his Thursday-morning starter duties. He was coaching Curtis Strange, the Virginian who had been leading the Masters the previous year until his round imploded on the back nine on Sunday. Fans begged Snead to hit a few, but instead the Slammer moved on to chat with Raymond Floyd, who had earned his green jacket in 1976. Finally giving in to the fans' entreaties, Snead picked out Floyd's 3-iron and hit a picture-perfect shot out to the range, his form almost identical to what it was in the 1930s.

There was time for more fun at the Par 3 Contest. A 1,060-yard course—par 27, of course, played over DeSoto Springs Pond and Ike's Pond—had been built by Clifford Roberts and architect George Cobb in 1958. Two years later, the first Par 3 Contest was held, and it was won by Snead. Over the years, players in that year's Masters, noncompeting past Masters champions, and honorary guests of the Tournament Committee were invited to participate. In the twenty-five years that the contest had been held, no winner of it had gone on to win the tournament. (The so-called jinx has continued to this day.)

This was too bad for Gary Koch, who won the contest over Augusta native Larry Mize after three extra holes. One highlight was the hole-in-one recorded by Gary Player at the 7th. Another was the outfit of Payne Stewart, who wore a black tie and starched shirt to go with his black knickers.

There was not much in the way of festivities on Wednesday night. The days of Jimmy Demaret, who had the unique ability to combine partying with winning three green jackets, were over. Jack Nicklaus, like the other players, would stay in that night and focus on a good night's sleep. It was twenty-seven years since his first Masters and twenty-three years since he had first won at Augusta National, so Nicklaus knew what was necessary to prepare to play.

Even if, as many were saying or at least thinking, he was too old to win one more Masters, Jack wanted to give a good account of himself on the national stage.

4

It was appropriate that while the Masters was at the half-century mark, the course was in almost full bloom, symbolizing that Augusta National was still in its prime as one of the great challenges in golf. In 1986 it was just the right place to put on display the tectonic shift that was underway in the sport: the unprecedented combination of a supremely talented new generation of American players and an influx of foreign players that dramatically raised the level of competition.

Many of the players who had become big stars in the 1960s through the mid-1980s, as television helped golf surge in popularity, were still active—among them Billy Casper, Gene Littler, Tony Jacklin, Lee Trevino, Chi Chi Rodriguez, Johnny Miller, Tom Watson, Raymond Floyd, Ben Crenshaw, Hale Irwin, and Tom Weiskopf, as well as Palmer, Player, and Nicklaus. Some were still winning on the PGA Tour. Watson, in particular, had enjoyed a dominating, Nicklaus-like decade: since 1977, when he turned twenty-seven, he had won a U.S. Open and two Masters, and he had triumphed at the British Open five times, eclipsing Walter Hagen as the American with the most Claret Jugs.

Other well-known American golfers were taking advantage of the seeming lifetime annuity being offered by the Senior PGA Tour. Palmer had won the PGA Seniors Championship, the first major on that tour he had been eligible to play in after turning fifty, and his popularity gave the senior circuit immediate credibility. A victory by any of these names on either tour resulted in back-page headlines, highlights shown on news broadcasts and the new cable network ESPN, and plenty of watercooler and barroom conversation.

But the players of the next generation were emerging, all in their twenties and early thirties, and all were on hand in Augusta in April 1986. Lanny Wadkins had taken the PGA Championship in 1977 and was already a clutch player on the U.S. Ryder Cup team. Fuzzy Zoeller had shocked everyone (including himself) by winning the Masters on his first try in 1979, in a playoff over Ed Sneed and the piping hot Watson; five years later he won the U.S. Open. The burly and mustached Craig Stadler, nicknamed Walrus, had won the green jacket in 1982. Hal Sutton had captured the PGA Championship cup—the Wanamaker Trophy—in 1983. Two months earlier, Larry Nelson had won the U.S. Open at Oakmont, edging a frustrated Watson by a stroke.

Also grinding up leaderboards were young players such as Chip Beck, Corey Pavin, Payne Stewart, Bob Tway, Mark Calcavecchia, Larry Mize, Calvin Peete, Paul Azinger, Scott Verplank, Tom Kite, Mark O'Meara, Jeff Sluman, Peter Jacobsen, Curtis Strange, and enough others to fill up any locker room. As they crowded into the upper level of the PGA Tour money list, they left little room for the aging heroes.

That was one significant reason for the change in golf. The other reason came from overseas.

It could be said that the Masters was the most American of the four modern majors. The British Open was completely dominated by English and Scottish players for sixty-two years, until Walter Hagen became the first American-born golfer to seize the Claret Jug in 1922. The U.S. Open, too, saw only English and Scottish champions from its founding in 1895 until 1911, when Johnny McDermott, just nineteen years old, won the tournament at the Chicago Golf Club. When the PGA Championship was founded in 1916, as the showcase event for the Professional Golfers' Association, which had been formed in New York City earlier in the year, many of the PGA players were immigrants to America, such as Jim Barnes, who won the first Wanamaker Trophy that October.

During the 1920s, U.S. players ascended to the best in the world, led by Hagen, Sarazen, and Jones. Hagen won his five PGA Championships—fully half of those held in the decade. It was a phenomenal feat considering that the format of the event at the time was match play, and a defeat in any match meant being eliminated from the tournament. (From 1924 to 1928, when he was finally dethroned by Leo Diegel, Hagen won twenty-two consecutive matches.) Sarazen won the U.S. Open in 1922, and Jones won it four times before his retirement in 1930. Even the British Open wasn't immune: between them, Hagen and Jones won it seven times from 1922 to 1930.

By the time of that first Masters in 1934, the majority of the better players in the United States were Americans, and it would remain that way into the 1980s. America's record in the Ryder Cup reflected that. The biennial team event was cofounded by Samuel Ryder and Walter Hagen after an exhibition match in England in 1926, and the first official contest was held the following year in Worcester, Massachusetts. The U.S. team, led by Hagen and Sarazen, won easily. Great Britain won at home in 1929, and the U.S. and British teams continued to trade home-soil victories in the next three contests. But after the United States won in 1935, it did not lose again until the 1957 Ryder Cup match in England. There was a tie in 1969, also in England, but the next U.S. loss wasn't until 1985 at the Belfry, again in England. More often than not, the Yanks won by healthy margins. Perhaps the strongest team of that pre-1985 period was one captained by PGA Championship winner Dave Marr in 1981 that had on its roster, in addition to Nicklaus and Watson, Ben Crenshaw, Raymond Floyd, Hale Irwin, Tom Kite, Bruce Lietzke, Johnny Miller, Larry Nelson, Jerry Pate, Bill Rogers, and Lee Trevino. It won easily, 18½ to 9½.

The era of unchallenged American dominance was coming to an end, however. After a typical lopsided U.S. triumph in 1977, Jack Nicklaus lobbied the PGA of America and its counterpart across the pond to amend the original charter created by Ryder and Hagen to allow the British team to include players from elsewhere in Europe. Two years later, the first all-Europe team took to the Greenbrier course in West Virginia. They were defeated, however, and then there was the 1981 drubbing.

But a shift in the balance of power could be seen at the 1983 Ryder Cup Match at the PGA National Golf Club in Florida, where the home team would have suffered an upset if not for some late-Sunday heroics by Wadkins and Watson that had Nicklaus, the captain, kissing the ground in gratitude. The Americans barely won, 14½ to 13½. In 1985 the United States had a formidable team once more, but the European lineup was by far the best ever. It included Nick Faldo of England, Ian Woosnam of Wales, Sandy Lyle of Scotland, Seve Ballesteros from Spain, and Bernhard Langer from West Germany. The Europeans not only broke through with a victory, 16½ to 11½ at the Belfry, but in another example of no good deed going unpunished, two years later Nicklaus would suffer the fate of being the first U.S. Ryder Cup captain to lose on American soil. To make it worse, the 15-to-13 shocker happened at what had become his home course, one he designed and built, Muirfield Village in Ohio.

"When the Europeans won the Ryder Cup in the fall of '85, all of us on the PGA Tour realized that the players on that team were going to be a force to be reckoned with, especially in future team events," recalls Tom Kite, who was a member of the U.S. squad that year. "We still felt like we had the better individual players who would win more tournaments and especially the majors. This, obviously, proved to be incorrect as Sandy, Ian, Bernhard, Nick, and Seve, among others, made their presence felt."

Strong signals of the foreign emergence extended to Augusta, beginning with the dawn of the 1980s. Though only twenty-three, Seve Ballesteros played brilliant golf the second week in April 1980, coasting to a four-stroke victory. He carded a 275 total to earn the green jacket and by so doing denied Nicklaus an even closer brush with the modern Grand Slam that year, as Jack went on to win the U.S. Open and PGA Championship. To put an exclamation mark on his triumph, Ballesteros became the youngest Masters champion, had the lowest seventy-two-hole total by an international player, and was the only foreign-born golfer other than Gary Player to win the Masters.

Three years later, he was back in the winner's circle. Two years after that, in 1985, Bernhard Langer was presented with the first-place check. For the 1986 Masters, both champions had returned, and among the other European players flexing their muscles were Nick Faldo, Jose Maria Olazabal, Ian Woosnam, and Sandy Lyle, who had won the Greensboro Open the week before the Masters and the previous July had become the first British subject in sixteen years to win that nation's Open.

The foreign invasion into U.S. golf was led by talented and confident non-Europeans too. While he was not the only such golfer to be found on the PGA Tour in the 1960s and 1970s, by far the most prominent and successful had been South Africa's Gary Player. In 1957 his father had written a letter to Clifford Roberts requesting an invitation to the Masters for his son. The elder Player said that he would take up a collection at the local club in South Africa to pay Gary's expenses. Intrigued, Roberts issued the invitation with the response "Pass the hat." Only four years later, Player became the first non-American Masters champion. He had plenty of top-ten finishes in the event, and he won again at Augusta in 1974 and 1978. While he was becoming a fan favorite there, the frequent flyer was compiling one of the greatest careers in golf with 24 PGA Tour victories, a total of 163 worldwide tournament wins, and 9 majors.

By 1986, Player was far from the only non-European foreigner with recognition in America. Dubious renown, however, belonged to Argentina's Roberto De Vicenzo, who had finished the 1968 Masters tied for first place with Bob Goalby. Playing partner Tommy Aaron had put down an incorrect number on De Vicenzo's scorecard, and the Argentine had signed it. When the error was discovered, he was assessed a two-stroke penalty and thus was second to Goalby, who was awarded the green jacket. The crushed De Vicenzo repeated forlornly, "What a stupid I am!"

Australian Greg Norman, nicknamed the Shark, with his NFL quarterback build and flowing white-blond mane, was rising up the ranks toward becoming the number one golfer in the world. (In the summer of 1986, he would win the first of his two British Opens and finish second in both the U.S. Open and PGA Championship.) He had tied for first in the 1984 U.S. Open and then lost in a playoff to Fuzzy Zoeller, who earned his second major in his first five seasons on the tour. (Alas, it was to be his last.)

Nick Price, who had been born in what was then Rhodesia (later Zimbabwe), was showing flashes of brilliance. He had burst on the PGA Tour three years earlier with a win at the World Series of Golf. Denis Watson, like Price born in Rhodesia, also showed promise. From Japan was Tsuneyuki "Tommy" Nakajima, and from Taiwan was T. C. Chen, who had finished second in the U.S. Open the year before. And the veteran David Graham of Australia had the hardware to show for winning the U.S. Open in 1981 and a PGA Championship in 1979. Of the eighty-eight players entered in the 1986 Masters, twelve were foreign.

But what made the foreign players especially worthy of headlines, aside from winning four of the last eight Masters, were two controversies that had recently intensified: the issue of taxes, and the players' growing confidence, which some American fans saw as cockiness.

According to an Internal Revenue Service formula in 1986, if a foreign player spent more than 120 days in the United States, his worldwide earnings would be subject to taxation. Say a foreign player is having a good year and has won $100,000 in the United States and $150,000 in tournaments elsewhere in the world. If he is in the United States for 120 days or less, only the $100,000 is taxed. But if he stays longer, the IRS will collect taxes on the full $250,000—even if the $150,000 from international earnings has already been taxed by his home country.

What made the rules especially difficult was that every day spent in the United States counted toward the deadline, even days when the foreign player skipped a tournament and earned no money. Langer, for example, had participated in eleven straight tourneys by the beginning of April 1986, ten of them in the United States. With five top-ten finishes, including losing in a playoff to Bob Tway at the Andy Williams Open in February, Langer had earned $160,515 and was fifth on the PGA Tour money list. Then he took a break by not playing in the Greensboro Open the week before the Masters, but he was still in the United States, so the layoff counted toward his tax deadline.

Foreign players faced a catch-22: According to PGA Tour rules, they had to play in fifteen tournaments to keep their tour card. But entering that many events guaranteed that they would be in the United States for more than 120 days. Thus, foreign players were forced to choose between their cards and their tax burdens.

"It changes your life," the understated Langer said at the beginning of Masters week. "By the time the Masters ends, I will already be here ninety-seven days."

As a result, Langer said, even if he repeated as Masters champion, he would play in only three more tournaments and then be done for the year in the United States. West Germany taxed his total income, including what he earned in the States, so after 120 days he would have two different countries taxing the same total.

The conundrum for the United States, on the other hand, was that right at the time that foreign stars such as Norman, Faldo, and Ballesteros were further galvanizing golf and the audiences (and purses) were growing, the IRS formula was limiting the number of events these players could participate in. Organizations behind the two other majors didn't have to worry too much—the U.S. Open and the PGA Championship were two of the three events Langer would play, for example—but as the year went on at least a dozen or more other tourneys would have to make do with such nonmarquee names as Wayne Levi, Rick Fehr, and David Ogrin instead of the top-shelf international players.

Ballesteros had taken a different tack than Langer: instead of fretting over making too much money or staying too many days in the United States, in 1985 he decided to play in only nine PGA Tour events. For that he was suspended by Deane Beman, the PGA Tour commissioner. The PGA had no jurisdiction over the Masters, and Ballesteros was already eligible as the owner of two green jackets, but the only other event he'd been allowed to play in to that point in 1986 was the USF&G Classic in New Orleans. There he missed the cut by a stroke, meaning that in the three-plus months leading to the Masters he had all of two rounds of competitive golf in the United States to prepare him. So little competitive play in itself meant that, despite Ballesteros's great talent, winning the Masters would be an uphill battle. But adding to his burden was the fact that in March his father, Baldomero, had succumbed to cancer, which hit the youngest of four sons hard.

Defiantly, the Spaniard told anyone who would listen, "Beman is a little man who wants to be big" and "I've had some problems with him in the past.

Maybe he had a chance to do something against me and maybe that makes him happy."

His wry sense of humor broke through when he added, "I have no problems with taxes here this year. I haven't made any money."

That would change on Wednesday afternoon when he and Gary Player defeated David Graham and Ben Crenshaw in a practice round and collected fifty dollars each, bringing Ballesteros's total earnings in practice play that week to ninety dollars. Obviously, he did not share Langer's income tax issues.

But both men, and their fellow European stars, shared a confidence bordering on cockiness. Langer and Ballesteros could afford it—they had green jackets in their closets. (Actually, winners' jackets were kept hanging and waiting for them year-round in the Augusta National locker room.) "I'm really here to win the tournament," Langer stated on Wednesday. "I'm not here to play for places, to finish in the top twenty-four. I'm not going to lay up. I'm going to attack the course."

Ballesteros had done the West German one better the day before, his twenty-ninth birthday. Already the winner of four majors, with two British Open victories and two Masters triumphs, Seve convincingly proclaimed, "I am ready to win. I'm talking serious. I'm ready. Of course, you cannot be 100 percent, but close." And when he was asked about how holes 16 through 18 on Sunday would affect the outcome, Ballesteros predicted, "The tournament will be over by then."

He had no concerns about his lack of competitive play. Ballesteros emphasized that he was a two-time Masters champion who had tied for second in 1985, and said: "I feel very strong mentally and physically. I came here to win the Masters."

He was voicing what many of the foreign players felt.

5

Though Thursday was another sunny, dry day, the stiff southwesterly breeze had turned into a full-blown wind, and whenever it gusted as high as twenty-five miles per hour, it caused many players problems. Those who had gone out early had the advantage of some softness on the greens, but by noon they were quite dry.

As prepared as Jack Nicklaus was to begin the first round of the Masters, he had to be wondering what would happen that day, given his play in 1986 so far. Getting off to a good start was as important now, if not more so, as it was when he was in the majors and still the man to beat, and on the brighter side of forty-five.

But Nicklaus was aggravated by a putter that wouldn't cooperate. On the front nine his tee shots were fine, his iron play even better, but getting the ball to drop into the cup was frustrating. He was over par at the turn.

He was not alone, though. As the greens dried, many of the players found that some of their most carefully struck putts went awry. A good example was Fred Couples on the second hole. The twenty-six-year-old was nick-named Boom-Boom because of his prodigious tee shots, and on this par-5 hole he was on the green in two. He had what looked like a very makeable ten-footer for eagle, and he tapped the ball gently. It missed the hole, and as he and the patrons watched in dismay, it kept going for another forty feet. The adventure had a very happy conclusion, however, because Couples sank that second putt for a birdie, and he offered the spectators a wry smile. Most of his fellow competitors had little to smile about; like Nicklaus, they were struggling to stay at or near par early in their rounds.

The tee time for Arnold Palmer on Thursday morning was 10:01. He approached the tee box four minutes early, welcomed with warm applause. There were members of the crowd who had seen Palmer first play at Augusta in 1954, and they had grown older together every April since.

"When I look at them, I see most of the same faces I've seen out there for the last thirty years," he said later. "It's just nice to know that. Sure, the chances for my winning aren't good, but the spirit of it is still there. That's awfully nice."

Palmer bowed under the rope and into the tee area like a boxer entering the ring. Without yet carding a score, he was in the Masters to win it as much as Ballesteros or any of the other players. Heck, in the first round in 1983, he had opened with a 68. Probably he was a tad shorter than many remembered, the hair was now thinner and white, and he wore a hearing aid, but he was still compactly built. He wore a lime-green shirt and an azure cashmere sweater and a smile for the gallery. There were very few Pennsylvanians here in Augusta, but they were still his people.

His drive landed in the left rough, among a stand of pine trees. After a familiar hitch of his pants, Palmer sent his second shot up and through the trees. The ball landed short of the green. It would be that kind of day. His tee shot on the par-3 fourth hole skipped into heavy brush, and he bogeyed. He three-putted from sixteen feet on the sixth hole.

The round wasn't going well at all. But Palmer gamely played on, and there were still exhortations from the crowd as though this was a tournament from twenty years ago. Arnie smiled back—it was a pretty day, and he was back in Augusta. No major had been as kind to him as the Masters.

6

To this day, Jack Nicklaus remains one of the most recognizable sports figures in the world. His victories overseas, including the three British Opens, brought him international renown, and projects undertaken by his golf design company and other businesses can be found all over the globe. Yet his story is very much an American one, and it began when a European made his way to the heartland of the United States.

Peter Nicklaus had lived in eastern France as the 1800s began. His grandchildren immigrated to the United States and settled in Kansas and Ohio. One of them was Jack's great-grandfather, who founded the Nicklaus Boiler Works in Columbus, Ohio. His son, Louis, followed in his footsteps, and he and his wife, Arkie, had five children; the second one was Jack's father, Louis Charles Nicklaus, who would be known to everyone as Charlie.

Charlie Nicklaus was born in Columbus in 1913. Charlie loved playing sports—football in high school; football, basketball, and baseball at Ohio State; and tennis, golf, and hunting and fishing as much as work would allow in his adult years. That love, and the admiration he had formed for Bobby Jones as a thirteen-year-old in 1926 at the Scioto Country Club, he would pass on to his son.

"Our deepest bond, from my earliest memory of Dad, was our passionate love of sports," Nicklaus wrote in *Jack Nicklaus: My Story*. "Looking back now, I sometimes wonder how my mother, Helen, and my younger sister, Marilyn, tolerated the pair of us."

Charlie Nicklaus stayed in Columbus after college and became a pharmacist. He and his wife had two children, the first being Jack William Nicklaus, born on January 21, 1940.

The Nicklaus family was middle-class. They never had to miss a meal or worry about having a roof over their heads, but they were not wealthy, either. Charlie worked hard to build up the family business, and eventually he would own and operate six drugstores, which allowed the family to move to the Columbus suburb of Upper Arlington.

When Charlie was in his early thirties, he broke a bone in his ankle while playing volleyball. After surgery, in 1949, he was advised to stick to mild exercise for a while. He was already a member, for social purposes, of the Scioto Country Club, so he began gingerly playing golf there, a few holes at a stretch.

"Knowing my readiness to try anything sporting, he invited me to caddie for him," Nicklaus recalled. "We would amble through a hole or two, then, using a few cut-down clubs, I'd amuse myself on a green or in a bunker while he rested. I enjoyed doing pretty much anything with my father, so this was fine by me."

An unforeseen byproduct of Charlie's rehab was the emergence of his son's true talent, and he nurtured it. At the age of only ten and playing his first nine holes at Scioto, Jack shot a 51. Golf was not the only sport he played during his school years—football and especially baseball were favorites—but it was the sport he couldn't help excelling at. He was twelve when he earned the Ohio State Junior Championship, and, robbing any other youngsters in Ohio of the opportunity, he took the title four straight times after that.

A great golf career was almost nipped in the bud when both thirteen-year-old Jack and his younger sister contracted polio. For him, it was a milder case, and his strength and athleticism allowed him to recover fully.

At fourteen, he won the Tri-State High School Championship, which brought together young golfers from Kentucky and Indiana as well as Ohio.

The following year he set the course record at Scioto for an amateur with a 66. The year after that he won the Ohio Open, carding a 64 in the third round and indicating he was already at least the equal of any professionals in the state. By winning twenty-seven events between the ages of ten and seventeen, Jack Nicklaus made it clear that golf was *the* sport for him.

Besides Jack's father and their idol Bobby Jones, Jack Grout was another influence. Born in Oklahoma and raised in Texas, Grout had played golf professionally but had won only two tournaments eight years apart, and with back trouble bedeviling him, he became a teaching professional. By 1950, Grout was a pro at Scioto, and that June, Jack Nicklaus signed up for his junior golf class.

Grout became the most important teacher, mentor, and friend in Jack's young life, aside from his father. The youngster couldn't work hard enough for him, and that impressed Grout. Even during the Ohio winter, Nicklaus wrote, "I'd hit Jack's teaching balls, then my own practice balls, then I'd borrow everyone else's I could find around the club. At snowy times I would wait for the thaw, then go out and pick up all the balls, then go to work all over again. I'm sure some of the older members thought I was mentally impaired, even downright crazy. They probably thought the same about Jack Grout, too, for standing out there in the cold with me."

In 1955, when he was fifteen, Jack qualified for his first U.S. Amateur Championship, but he was defeated by Bob Gardner in the first round. The following year he made it to the third round, then lost 3 and 2 to Ronnie Wenzler. In 1957 the Amateur Championship was held at the Country Club in Brookline, Massachusetts, the site of Francis Ouimet's triumph in the U.S. Open forty-four years earlier. Nicklaus made it to the fourth round this time but lost by the same 3 and 2 score to Dick Yost. The next year, two-time Amateur champion Harvie Ward downed Nicklaus on the last hole in the second round. As good as he was in other events, Jack couldn't get to the Amateur finals, and in 1958 he seemed to be going backward.

A consolation was that, at seventeen, he earned a spot in the 1957 U.S. Open being played in Ohio, at the Inverness Club. Shooting an abysmal 160, Jack didn't make the cut—neither did Arnold Palmer, who shot a 152—but the 1957 tournament, won by Dick Mayer in a playoff over Cary Middlecoff, was the first of what would be forty-four consecutive appearances in the U.S. Open for Jack.

At eighteen, he played in his first PGA Tour event, tying for twelfth in the Rubber City Open in Akron, Ohio, and he made his first cut in a U.S. Open, winding up forty-first in the 1958 edition at Southern Hills in Oklahoma, which featured the top three finishers Tommy Bolt, Gary Player, and Julius Boros. But at the 1959 Open at Winged Foot he regressed again, shooting a 154 and missing the cut.

Jack was seriously thinking about emulating his hero Jones and remaining an amateur indefinitely, so his immediate holy grail, especially after his latest Open disappointment, was the next Amateur Championship. It was to be held at the Broadmoor Golf Club in Colorado in September 1959.

He was met with an emotional as well as competitive challenge in the first round: Jack's opponent was Robert Jones III, son of his golf idol. Sentiment, however, did not prevent Jack from dusting Jones 7 and 6. His next match was a close win, 2 and 1, followed by another runaway, 6 and 5. In the next round he won another tight match, 1-up, and a 3 and 1 win in the quarterfinals meant for the first time Jack had advanced to the semifinals.

There he faced Gene Andrews, a Los Angeles golfer in his forties who five years earlier had won the Public Links Championship, a national event. It was a thirty-six-hole seesaw battle, with Jack up at eighteen holes, then down, then up, then down. He was up 1 with two holes to play. His twenty-five-footer halved the seventeenth hole, and after another halve, Jack had won 1-up.

In the final, Jack faced a daunting opponent. Charlie Coe of Oklahoma had just captained the U.S. Walker Cup team and was the reigning Amateur champion; he had first won the title in 1949. That April in the Masters, Coe had finished in sixth place, as the top amateur. After eighteen holes, Jack was down 2. Not until 12, the thirtieth hole, did he pull even; six holes would determine the championship. They remained deadlocked.

On 18, they hit 3-woods off the tee, and Nicklaus's ball stopped rolling six feet ahead of his opponent's. Coe hit an 8-iron that looked perfect, but his ball didn't bite on the green and went over the back edge. Displaying the maturity that would characterize his play in pressure moments early in his career, Nicklaus learned from that shot. He put away his 8-iron and played a semipunch shot with a 9-iron. His ball stopped eight feet from the hole. Coe pitched back up to the green. After conceding the tap-in putt, Jack had that eight-footer to win the match. "From the moment it left the blade it was never in doubt," was Jack's laconic description in *Jack Nicklaus: My Story*. He had won his first national title.

Earning top honors at the U.S. Amateur Championship meant that Jack was automatically in the 1960 U.S. Open, to be played at the Cherry Hills Country Club outside Denver. Making the cut there wouldn't be enough—he had already done that in an Open championship. Instead, he hoped to be noticed by being within shouting distance of the leaderboard after seventy-two holes. Well, he had just had a good experience in Colorado—perhaps he could have another one.

7

In 1935 the best American golfer was Gene Sarazen. Bobby Jones had been retired for five years. Walter Hagen's last hurrah was earning his fifth Western Open title in 1932 (then considered a quasi-major) at age thirty-nine; he was now fading fast, and the Gasparilla Open in 1935 would be his last solo win on tour. No one else had Sarazen's resume: U.S. Open wins in 1922 and 1932, a British Open victory in 1932, and PGA Championships in 1922, 1923, and 1933. He was a fierce competitor who could have easily won a couple more majors if the ball had bounced the right way.

Though only thirty-three, he was viewed as part of an older generation because of his jousts with Jones and Hagen (and his stubborn insistence on wearing knickers while a younger generation of golfers was switching to pants). Sarazen kept the promise he had made to Jones and Roberts the previous year, when he couldn't attend, that he would be in Augusta for the 1935 Augusta National Invitation Tournament—the second-ever Masters. Thus that generation's triumvirate was assembled to compete for the first time since the 1930 U.S. Open in Minnesota, at which Jones had won and Hagen and Sarazen had finished seventeenth and twenty-eighth, respectively.

Ordinarily, this would have caused much excitement, but 1935 was smack in the middle of the Depression decade, and the golf circuit was hurting. This was especially true of the Masters, which was already on fragile financial footing. The number of participants was sixty-five, down seven from 1934. The club lost money conducting the Masters in 1935, but if Augusta National was to even exist, Roberts and Jones could not suspend the event after just one year. And golf fans did pay attention—especially after they learned of the outcome, which featured what has often been called the greatest golf shot ever.

Sarazen had played well the first three rounds, but not well enough to be in first place. Craig Wood held the lead. In the final round, he had the Squire by three strokes and was already in the clubhouse ready to accept the winner's check. Sarazen teed off on the par-5 fifteenth hole, and when he approached his ball on the fairway he didn't like what he saw. The ball was sitting down in a bad lie, and he still had 235 yards to the pin. His caddie suggested a 3-wood. Sarazen was inclined toward a 4-wood. The decision time stretched longer and longer.

Here Hagen played a crucial role. He and Sarazen were close friends, yet they also knew how to push each other's buttons. The thirty-six-hole final match between the two for the PGA Championship in Pelham, New York, in 1923 was bitterly contested—Hagen was the 1921 champion, Sarazen the defending champion. They played mind games on each other long before anyone knew or cared about sports psychology. On the sixth hole, Hagen had a putt of only a foot, and he expected Sarazen to concede it. Instead, the twenty-one-year-old growled, "Hole it. I'm giving you nothing but hell today."

In the final round of the 1935 Masters, Hagen was Sarazen's playing partner. As the Squire vacillated, the Haig became impatient. That it was five-thirty on a chilly afternoon didn't help, and he had plans. Finally, Hagen shouted, "Hurry up, will ya? I've got a date tonight!"

That did it. Sarazen angrily grabbed the 4-wood and slammed the ball. It soared toward the flag, then went in for a double eagle, tying him with Wood, who like everyone else in the clubhouse was stunned to hear the news. The fourth round ended with him and Sarazen, who had parred the last three holes, in a tie. Sarazen won the next day's thirty-six-hole playoff—the only two-round playoff in Masters history—and the winner's check that had almost been in Wood's hands was his, plus a fifty-dollar bonus for the playoff. (The ball that Sarazen holed continues to be on display at Augusta National.) With this victory, Sarazen became the first man to complete what would become known as the modern Career Grand Slam. Of more immediate significance were the headlines his miracle shot spawned. They informed more people about the beautiful course in a corner of Georgia and its annual invitational—which was already being referred to as "the Masters."

Some might think that founding a tournament and calling it the Masters is rather presumptuous. And it would be. But that wasn't what happened at Augusta National.

The name "Masters" had been used in print as early as the first tournament, notably by sportswriter Grantland Rice. But Roberts and especially Jones were uncomfortable with the name. It could be perceived as pretentious, and given the unsteady origins of the event, perhaps it promised more than it could produce. But every year, the term appeared in print and on the lips of players and spectators more often, and in 1938 Roberts and Jones made "the Masters" official for the following spring's tournament.

The club struggled through the 1930s, with Roberts somehow finding ways to pay the most pressing bills while endeavoring to keep his own Wall Street career afloat. The good news was that the better players kept showing up every year, and a tradition grew.

And some very good golf was played. Inaugural Masters champion Horton Smith won the tournament again in 1936, and the following year, winning his first major, was Byron Nelson. Henry Picard won in 1938, and in 1939 Ralph Guldahl bettered Wood and Sarazen's 1935 total of 282 by three shots to establish a new scoring record.

The 1940 Masters served as the genesis of what would become the PGA Hall of Fame. That April, the golf writers in attendance discussed honoring players who had made significant contributions to the development and success of golf in the United States. Twelve men were nominated: Willie Anderson, four-time U.S. Open winner; Tommy Armour, who won one each of the U.S. Open, PGA Championship, and British Open; Jim Barnes, winner of the inaugural PGA Championship in 1916 and the U.S. Open in 1921; Chick Evans, the best American amateur after Bobby Jones and winner of the 1916 U.S. Open; Walter Hagen, who virtually created the occupation of professional golfer when, up to his 1919 Open win, the day job of most competitors was golf professional; Bobby Jones himself; Johnny McDermott, the first man born in the United States to win its national championship, in 1911 and 1912; Francis Ouimet, the amateur whose defeat of Harry Vardon and Ted Ray in the 1913 Open playoff resulted in a big leap in interest in golf in America; Sarazen, winner of seven majors; Alex Smith, three-time U.S. Open champion; Jerry Travers, another excellent player who remained an amateur and who won the 1915 U.S. Open; and Walter Travis, the "old man" who at forty-three became the first American to win the British Amateur, in 1904, and who went on to become the founding editor of the *American Golfer.*

These inductees composed an excellent beginning, but it would be another thirteen years before the second class, consisting of Ben Hogan, Sam Snead, and Byron Nelson, was inducted.

As World War II broke out in Europe, the Masters persevered. In 1940 the hottest player in the United States was Jimmy Demaret, he who partied almost as well as he played golf. (He stood in sharp contrast to his fellow Texan, Nelson, who didn't drink a drop.) Demaret had already won five tournaments in the young PGA season. But he had tied for thirty-third in his first Masters the year before, so he was not favored by many in the 1940 edition. His 280 total topped Lloyd Mangrum by four strokes, the first time the winning margin was larger than two at Augusta National.

Craig Wood, from whom Sarazen had snatched victory seven years earlier, finally broke through in 1941. He didn't win a green jacket, however, because that tradition wouldn't begin for another eight years. By 1942, the United States had declared war on Germany, Japan, and their allies, and many believed that the 1942 Masters would be the last one for a while— or forever, if World War II lasted long enough and the owners of Augusta National couldn't survive it.

If it was to be the last Masters, the tournament did not disappoint.

There, Byron Nelson said, he played the best golf of his career. This was a remarkable admission considering the season he'd had three years later, when he won nineteen of the thirty tournaments he entered—eighteen of them PGA events—and eleven of them in a row, and his stroke average for the year was 68.33.

But in that Masters of 1942, Nelson and the late-blooming Ben Hogan—who, unlike Nelson and Snead, had yet to win a major—finished tied after seventy-two holes. The next day, they were about to embark on an eighteen-hole playoff when Hogan learned that Nelson had been violently ill during the night and wasn't all that much better in the morning. Hogan suggested they postpone the playoff until later in the day or the next day. Nelson, who had known Hogan since they were adolescent caddies in Fort Worth—and had beaten him for the caddie championship at their club in a nine-hole playoff—declined.

Perhaps he should have accepted, because after only five holes, Lord Byron was down by three strokes. Then there was a sharp turnabout: Over the next stretch, through the thirteenth hole, Hogan was one under par—yet he lost five strokes. Nelson birdied the sixth, eleventh, twelfth, and thirteenth holes and eagled the eighth. A reeling Hogan plugged gamely on, but at the end of the day Nelson edged him 69 to 70 to earn his second Masters championship.

As war raged on, all of golf in the United States was affected. Many tournaments were put on hiatus, including the U.S. Open and the PGA Championship, and some of the players donned uniforms and headed to basic training. Jones was one of those who went off to war, leaving Roberts to run Augusta himself.

Augusta National, host of a tournament that had been held only nine times and was hanging precariously on a financial cliff, was especially vulnerable to the impact of war. Accepting this, Jones and Roberts made the decision to close the club after the 1942 tournament. If it turned out there would be no more Masters, at least the event had gone out with flying colors.

8

As soon as the PGA Championship ends in August, golf fans start looking ahead to the next major tournament, even though it is eight months away. That was certainly true during the winter of 1985–86: after Hubert Green nosed out Lee Trevino by two strokes at Cherry Hills to hold the Wanamaker Trophy aloft, the golf media and aficionados began to wonder if he was going to repeat in a major or if a more familiar name would collect the green jacket the following April, and if next year was finally going to be the one when a player captured a single-year Grand Slam.

The only player who had come close to the modern version of Jones's 1930 achievement was Ben Hogan. In 1953 he won at Augusta National with a blistering 274 total. He then earned a U.S. Open championship by a full six strokes over Sam Snead at Oakmont. Even more excitement was created when Hogan won his first and only British Open, at Carnoustie, where the crowd in Scotland dubbed him the Wee Ice Mon because of his serious demeanor. Given that he was mopping the course with his competitors, the Hawk, as he was also nicknamed, would have easily been the favorite to win the PGA Championship at the Birmingham Country Club in Michigan.

However, because of the unfriendly scheduling of the time, Hogan didn't even enter the event. It would have been almost impossible to get back from

Great Britain in time to tee off. And according to some, Hogan knew that even if he made it to the thirty-six-hole final match, he would not have been physically able to endure it, since he was still suffering lingering pain from a near-fatal 1949 accident in Texas, in which his car collided head-on with a bus. (The PGA winner in 1953 was Walter Burkemo, an unlikely obstacle to Hogan's drive for the slam, though a popular winner because as an army sergeant he had been wounded twice in the war.)

When Masters week begins, all kinds of scenarios are envisioned, and many of the participants are judged to be either odds-on favorites or long shots. In 1986 some writers hoped a local man would be fitted for a green jacket. The only Georgian who had ever won the Masters was Tommy Aaron in 1973; he had not done better than a tie for twenty-eighth after that, and in April 1986 he was the director of golf at a resort. Larry Nelson was also a Georgian and a fine player—in fact, in the 1984 Masters it looked like he might take the jacket, but on the twelfth hole he put a ball in Rae's Creek and wound up in a tie for fifth in the tournament won by Ben Crenshaw. Tom McCollister of the *Atlanta Journal-Constitution* dismissed Nelson's chances in 1986, writing that "he's playing awful. In his favor is temperament, course management and doggedness. Working against him is his putter, his suddenly poor iron play and inability to scramble."

Usually next on the list of hoped-for contenders are old favorites. In 1986, as popular as Jack Nicklaus with his five green jackets and Gary Player with his three were, for the fans nothing would be more exciting than a miracle from Arnold Palmer.

Palmer had won his first Masters in 1958 at age twenty-eight and, with odd regularity, had won every other year after that, donning his fourth and last green jacket in 1964. He was only thirty-four then, but he was confronted by the Nicklaus buzz saw—Nicklaus won in 1965 and 1966, and Palmer never won another major. Despite the confident assessment of his chances to have everything go right that one weekend in April 1986, only the biggest diehards in Arnie's Army in Augusta that week thought that at age fifty-six he had a ghost of a chance.

The closest any player had come to being an elder Masters champion was Hogan. In April 1967, he was fifty-four years old and his legs were so bad that some observers were comparing his hitch when he walked to Walter Brennan's on the TV show *The Real McCoys*. Yet on the Saturday of that Masters week, he played one of the best rounds of his life.

Bobby Jones was still alive then to see it, from his cabin adjacent to the tenth hole. Another member of that triumvirate, Gene Sarazen, was also at Augusta to witness it in person. The third member, Walter Hagen, watched what coverage was available on television in Michigan. On this Saturday, they witnessed the last hurrah for the Hogan-Snead-Nelson generation.

Hogan, easily noticeable in his white cap, had made the cut, a remarkable achievement in itself. After nine holes, he was even par. The fans, especially the nostalgic older ones, many of whom had watched the Hawk earn his last green jacket fourteen years earlier, were happy enough that he was holding his own after forty-five holes and that despite the pain he kept putting one foot in front of the other.

No one expected what came next, probably not even Hogan himself. On the tenth hole, the ball struck by his 7-iron came to rest seven feet from the hole. Birdie. At the eleventh, his 6-iron shot ended up just a foot shy of the cup. Birdie. He had a fifteen-footer at the twelfth. For years Hogan had been having an awful time with putting, yet he drained it for his third birdie in a row. His second shot with a 4-wood on the par-5 thirteenth hole also left him fifteen feet, and after two putts Hogan had another birdie. He parred three of the next four holes to be five under on the back nine.

The crowd had surged and was following him from hole to hole. The golfer was almost an apparition, a mythical hero from the distant past miraculously returned to life. At 18, his tee shot landed in the fairway. With deliberation, Hogan limped toward his ball. He struck it with a 5-iron and it landed on the green, but a good two dozen feet away. For a short man, he cast a tall shadow as he settled over the ball. He was still. There was utter silence in the gallery. Finally, the stroke. Birdie.

The Hawk, fourteen years after his last victory in a major, had shot a 30 on the back nine for a total of 66. Going into Sunday, he was only two strokes behind in the Masters, a tournament he had first played thirty years earlier.

As he sat in the clubhouse without his white cap, the reporters could see that Hogan was mostly bald now. He told them, according to Dave Kindred,

"There's a lot of fellas that have got to fall dead for me to win. But I don't mind telling you that I'll play just as hard as I've ever played in my life."

He did. But he was fifty-four and playing on aching legs that had given most of what they had left the day before. Hogan shot a 77 and finished in tenth place. Perhaps out of disappointment or a certainty that he would never contend at Augusta National again, he attended no more Tuesday-night Champions Dinners, the event he founded.

Back at the 1986 Masters, other favorites included Raymond Floyd and Tom Watson. Floyd had won the Masters with a brilliant 271 in 1976, but he was forty-three now and lumped into the same very dark-horse category as Lee Trevino, who had never won at Augusta, and Nicklaus. Watson had collected first-place checks in Augusta in 1977 and 1981 and was only thirty-six, but he was having putting problems. When Watson showed up in Augusta in April 1986, he, like Nicklaus, hadn't won a tournament in two years. As it turned out, his fifth British Open victory in 1983 would be his last major.

Most of the golf reporters and broadcasters put their money on the winner coming from this group: Fred Couples, Hal Sutton, Curtis Strange, Mark O'Meara, Lanny Wadkins, Tom Kite, Payne Stewart, and Calvin Peete. Of the amateurs, the best chance was given to Scott Verplank, who had won the venerable Western Open in a playoff in 1985. Somewhat guiltily, many of the prognosticators admitted that it would be no surprise if all of the Yanks were shut out and Seve Ballesteros, Bernhard Langer, or one of the other foreign players had the biggest grin on Sunday, April 13.

Recalls Pat Summerall, who anchored the 1986 Masters coverage by CBS, "When we had a meeting to map out which players we were likely to be spending the most time with, Jack's name wasn't even mentioned. I couldn't remember a Masters when that had happened before."

9

Was Jack Nicklaus really finished?

Those commentators and prognosticators who answered "Yes" pointed to three reasons why he had as much chance to win the 1986 Masters as the long-dead Harry Vardon. One was his game. In making only four of seven cuts, he had earned just $4,403 on the year thus far, and he said that "it cost me $100,000 to get there."

"Nobody was picking Nicklaus to win the Masters," recalled James Achenbach, who covered the 1986 tournament for *Golfweek*. "I remember throwing $10 into a Masters pool and watching with curiosity as Nicklaus remained unselected until one of the late rounds."

At the beginning of Masters week, Nick Seitz, a veteran writer and editor at golf magazines, interviewed several players for a radio program, and one question he asked was if Nicklaus might still prove a threat. Tom Kite stated that Nicklaus was "on the back side of his prime." Peter Jacobsen said that the Golden Bear had lost his putting confidence. (Indeed, his putting in the seven events he had entered in 1986 had him ranked 158th on the PGA Tour.) After similar comments by others, Seitz summed up Nicklaus's status for his audience: "His fellow pros no longer fear him."

For some of the younger ones, in fact, he was already a bit of a memory. "I think the players now respect him more for what he has done and what he has meant to golf than they respect him for his game," said Corey Pavin, twenty-six and in his third season on the PGA Tour. "If I was going head-to-head with him, I wouldn't be afraid of him or fear anything supernatural. I think when he was playing ten years ago he was a man to fear because of the way he was playing."

Nicklaus didn't seem to have lost his confidence, though. He told the Atlanta sports columnist Furman Bisher, "I've made four of seven cuts, and one [tournament] I had to leave when Barbara's mother [his mother-in-law] died. I've been hitting the ball well but hitting only nine or ten greens. That means I've been getting in a lot of practice on my short game. It hasn't been my putting. I've been putting well."

With another reporter, Nicklaus was downright defiant: "I still want to win and I think I can win. If nothing else, I'm going to do it just to show you guys I can still win."

The reporter, Glenn Sheeley of the *Atlanta Journal-Constitution* wrote, "Maybe so, but the consensus here is that a Nicklaus victory in the 1986 Masters would be comparable to what the U.S. hockey team did to the Russians in 1980. Because Nicklaus has so often been in boardrooms or behind a speaker's podium, instead of on a practice tee or a putting green, his game would have to improve for a finish such as 1985—sixth place, four shots back." Sheeley's allusion to Nicklaus's pursuits off the course was echoed by Calvin Peete, who told Seitz, "Maybe he doesn't have the time anymore."

These pursuits included being involved in charitable foundations; contributing articles to magazines, with the help of longtime friend Ken Bowden; writing books with Bowden, including the best seller *Golf My Way* (he had written his first autobiography, with Herbert Warren Wind, in 1969); making instructional videos; serving as a two-time Ryder Cup captain; and constructing and owning Muirfield Village Golf Club and running the annual Memorial Tournament there.

Nicklaus had always had strong business interests, especially course design, that had made him one of the wealthiest athletes in the world. Keeping up with all of them required significant multitasking, but he seemed to thrive on it. His generation had expanded the scope of a professional golfer's career. "I didn't have to talk to any sponsors, I just went out and played,"

Byron Nelson explained at Augusta National during the 1986 tournament. "Now you play three or four tournaments in a row, with all the other things that go along with it, you have to go home for a while to rest. Nicklaus has got so many things going, I don't know how he plays at all."

Recently, though, business matters had suddenly become much more than mere distractions for Nicklaus. "In the summer of 1985, at the age of forty-five, and with the belief that twenty-three years of building one of the best records in the history of golf had brought me a comfortable measure of financial security, came a severe shock," he wrote in *Jack Nicklaus: My Story*. "Out of the blue I was informed that both the company and I personally were so deeply in debt and at risk in real-estate and other non-golf-related projects as to face imminent financial disaster."

Everything Nicklaus had accumulated was in jeopardy, and that included his family's nest egg. To save the situation, he had to become more involved in his business ventures, which left less time for competitive golf.

In fact, on the Sunday before Masters week began, Nicklaus was at one of his newest course construction projects, the Country Club of the South in Georgia, observing bulldozers tearing up the red earth. "In a couple of hours he would shift into Masters gear, like Clark Kent in the phone booth," Furman Bisher reported. "He would fly to Augusta, switch into a Golden Bear shirt and become Super Jack. His public would hardly have recognized this fellow tramping through the woods and over the clods with a set of drawings in his hands and the worried look of a guy with a 40-foot putt for par."

At the same time, Nicklaus was also overseeing the construction of at least three other courses he had designed—the Country Club of Louisiana in Baton Rouge, Annandale in Mississippi, and Bear Creek in California. Beginning in the 1960s, when he joined Palmer as a client of the growing management firm IMG, founded by Mark McCormack, Nicklaus had always made a substantial amount of off-course golf revenue. But that was when he was in his twenties and thirties. Being tugged in different directions can be a lot more grueling at forty-six.

In a comment before the tournament that sounded harsher than he intended, Ken Venturi, the CBS analyst and winner of the 1964 U.S. Open, said about Nicklaus, "I haven't seen him play, because he hasn't been around to be on the air." Venturi added: "Jack's got to start thinking about when it is time to retire. He'd like to win again for everybody who said he was down and out, but, well, everybody would. The whole world is looking for Babe Ruth to hit another home run and Ben Hogan to shoot a 66."

There had been plenty of evidence already in 1986 that Jack was off his game. His tie for thirty-ninth at the Hawaiian Open in January was embarrassing mostly because it was his *best* performance of the year. Worse, however, was a tie for forty-seventh at the Doral Open in Florida only a few weeks before the Masters and failing to survive to Saturday and Sunday in three other tournaments.

Obviously, Nicklaus was struggling to make golf—especially championship-caliber golf—a priority in his life. If this tournament had not been the Masters, Nicklaus might have passed up playing the second week in April, or the entire month for that matter. But it was the Masters, and there was nowhere else he would rather be than at Augusta National, even though it seemed that everyone was counting the Golden Bear out.

10

It had to be hard for headline writers Thursday night, because the two top stories of the first round were Bill Kratzert and Ken Green, and neither would quicken the pulse of newspaper readers. Both had come out of nowhere to shoot 68.

You couldn't even credit their caddies for the players' sudden success.

Green's caddie was his sister, Shelley—who, her brother said cheerfully, "has no clue when it comes to golf." Two years earlier, bored with her job as an assistant bookkeeper in Connecticut, she offered to caddie for her younger brother, and Ken accepted. Of the 176 players and caddies on the field at Augusta National, she was the only woman. On the first practice day, she had to change in a van near the caddie shack. After that, however, Shelley was allowed to leave Augusta National with her uniform on, wash and dry it, and put it back on the next morning.

She had been on her brother's bag the previous August when he won the Buick Open, his only tour victory in four years. However, she told reporters at Augusta, instead of receiving the standard 5 percent of the winner's check, "He gave me a big kiss."

Bill Kratzert, meanwhile, drafted longtime friend Chuck Hofius, a regional sales manager for an electronics firm in Fort Wayne, Indiana, who had traveled to Augusta to show his support. On Wednesday afternoon,

Kratzert, a ten-year PGA Tour veteran known for having a short fuse, fired his regular caddie after the first nine holes of his practice round. Suddenly, Hofius, a 6-handicap, was on the bag for the last nine holes, and there he was again on the first tee Thursday morning. About Hofius, Kratzert quipped, "He came down to get a close look at the Masters, and I gave him a closer look than he ever imagined."

Like Green, Kratzert had one victory to his credit, the 1984 Pensacola Open, and he won a respectable $180,000 on tour in 1985, but maybe even his wife didn't expect him to be leading the Masters after eighteen holes. An excellent start helped: he rolled in a sixty-foot putt for birdie on the first hole.

Green put on an even more impressive putting exhibition. He sank a forty-footer for a birdie on the first hole, a seventy-footer on the fifth, and a fifty-footer on the sixteenth, and ended the round with another birdie putt, this one of only thirty-five feet.

It was almost divine intervention that they had scored so low. The dry, fast, windblown greens had most other players praying for lightning. Of the eighty-eight men in the Masters field, a mere fifteen broke par, and the field as a whole averaged 3.1 strokes over par. Heck, maybe Snead, Hogan, and Nelson shouldn't have retired from Masters competition—the septuagenarians couldn't have scored much worse.

For a while it had looked like Arnold Palmer was righting the ship, playing par golf, but then he had a double bogey on 10 and another on 12. The fans didn't care—those in the gallery nearest to the Sarazen Bridge on 15 gave Palmer a standing ovation. His playing partner, Garth McGimpsey, the British Amateur champion, wore the look of someone knowing and appreciating that he was playing with a legend.

When Palmer walked off the eighteenth green, he had rung up an 80. Instead of expressing disappointment, he looked forward to Friday's round. "I'm already thinking about what I have to shoot tomorrow to make the cut," said the man who was arguably the most popular golfer ever, rivaled only by the man who cofounded Augusta National. Maybe it could happen: Curtis Strange had shot an 85 in the first round in the previous year's Masters, and not only bounced back to make the cut but led the tournament for a while on Sunday. Strange, of course, hadn't been fifty-six.

Mac O'Grady had the unhappy distinction of recording the day's high round of 82, and that was with pars on 17 and 18. Better players weren't far behind: Hal Sutton was at 80, Lanny Wadkins at 78, the heralded amateur Scott Verplank at 77, and Hale Irwin at 76. Their caddies may have already been making travel plans for Friday night.

More bearable was a two-over-par 74, and among those who had shot that on Thursday were green-jacket owners Raymond Floyd, Craig Stadler, and Bernhard Langer. This time, Curtis Strange was at 73, one over on the day, and with another year of Augusta National experience, he had to be considered a contender through the weekend.

Along with Strange at one over par were Donnie Hammond, Fuzzy Zoeller, and Wayne Levi. As a past champion, Zoeller had to be given the edge to improve his position on Friday. At even par were Bill Glasson and Fred Couples. Given the wind and the condition of the greens, both young players had done well to keep their rounds intact.

Though not one of the leaders, Seve Ballesteros had played well enough and finished at 71, three strokes off the pace. That score was also carded by Ben Crenshaw, who had received his green jacket from Ballesteros two years earlier, and Hubert Green, Danny Edwards, Roger Maltbie, and Corey Pavin.

In the next group at 70 were five notable names—Greg Norman, Tommy Nakajima, Bob Tway, Tom Kite, and Tom Watson—and Dave Barr, a player from Canada. Watson's putting had really come through for him, and he had eagled the par-5 thirteenth hole.

With 69s, one stroke behind Bill Kratzert and Ken Green, were T. C. Chen and Gary Koch, the latter of whom had reason to believe he could defy the Par 3 Contest jinx. Of the ten men atop the leaderboard when Thursday's action ended, only Watson had previously won the Masters.

Jack Nicklaus, meanwhile, was another former champion who recorded a 74. On the back nine he had continued to strike the ball solidly and for the most part accurately off the tee, and he couldn't find much fault with his iron play.

Helping him every step of the way was his eldest son, Jackie. The twenty-four-year-old had played seriously himself, with some glimmers of his father's talent. He had been a member of the golf team at the University of North Carolina. He had won the North and South Amateur Championship. Inevitably, he hoped to win as a professional. He looked very much like his father, with a notable exception being that Jackie was a good five inches taller and did not have the middle-aged paunch his father had recently developed. (Watching Jack Nicklaus the day before on the practice tee, Herbert Warren Wind, on hand for the *New Yorker*, had observed, "He looked more like the Nicklaus of the 1965–70 period. It seemed that if he could make a few putts he might possibly put himself in the thick of the fight. On the other hand, he seemed to be considerably bulkier than he had been in some time.")

Jackie had caddied for his father at the Memorial Tournament in 1984, the last PGA Tour event that Jack had won. But Jackie couldn't help his father with his Achilles' heel: putting. His strength had always helped him on par-5s. That Thursday, he had made only one shot from within fifteen feet, and his only birdie of the day came on 13.

Six strokes off the lead wasn't good, but it wasn't too bad either. He had given a reasonably good account of himself under difficult conditions. Making the cut on Friday was a priority, but dwelling on it was pointless, because merely making the cut didn't put him in a position to win. And Jack still believed he would.

"Actually, I played very well today," he insisted after the end of play on Thursday. "The thing that has been bothering me all year has been my putting, and I couldn't get any in the hole today. I played very well. I drove the ball well. One bad shot all day. A bad shot at three and I made a bogey. Didn't have any bad shots. I think the way that I've been playing, if I can get some good shots, I can get some good scores."

Perhaps it's just as well he had no intention of reading the newspapers on Friday morning before teeing off and thus did not have to see writers giving a less-than-generous assessment of his first round. There were even writers who seemed to take some delight in remarking that with his recent poor play and a pedestrian 74 on Thursday, Jack was more Olden Bear than Golden Bear.

He would have dinner with Barbara and Jackie, then rest up to go for a lower score tomorrow. The forecast was good, and sunshine would warm up his forty-six-year-old bones.

THE SECOND ROUND

Friday, April 11

11

It must have seemed like a good idea at the time: turn Augusta National into a cattle ranch for the duration of World War II, a sort of Georgian Ponderosa, with Clifford Roberts as Ben Cartwright.

Because of gas rationing, players trading their plus-fours for military uniforms, and the wartime inevitability of less money available for purses, the PGA tour barely survived in 1943 and 1944. Golf did, however. To raise funds for the Red Cross, the USO, and other war-related organizations, exhibition matches were played around the country. Some featured well-known professional players, such as the Ryder Cup–like matches organized by the PGA of America that included Walter Hagen, Gene Sarazen, Craig Wood, and others. Bobby Jones did his share of exhibitions, too, until he entered the military, and there were fundraising duels with stars from other sports, such as Baseball Hall of Famers Babe Ruth and Ty Cobb, or from Hollywood, with duo Bing Crosby and Bob Hope of the *Road* comedies among the familiar big-screen faces participating.

But none of this would mean the reopening of Augusta National. So Jones came up with the idea of letting livestock roam the course. As the animals grazed, they would keep the growth of the grass under control in an inexpensive way, and selling them for food could provide a much-needed source of revenue. It was, as usual, Roberts's responsibility to make it happen.

And, as usual, he did. Soon, two hundred cattle and over fourteen hundred turkeys strolled the fairways where Lloyd Mangrum, Sam Snead, Paul Runyan, and other golfers once had. Unfortunately, for a variety of reasons, the price of beef plummeted in 1944, and the club lost five thousand dollars on the venture. (In his book *The Story of the Augusta National Golf Club*, Roberts contended that the turkey raising was a more successful enterprise that offset the cattle losses.) Better news was that upgrades and renovations to the course were made using German prisoners of war as laborers, and they didn't cost the club anything.

The end of the war in late summer 1945 brought some stability to Augusta's financial situation. More people joined the club, and some of the existing members whose businesses had done well during the war donated money or lent it on favorable terms. Renovations were made to the clubhouse, and two guest cottages were built; the one near the tenth-hole tee was built for Bobby Jones, to welcome him back from Europe.

While the infusion of funds was good news for Augusta National, Roberts was not certain if the club would hold a Masters Tournament anymore. In fact, given the past experiences, it might have been better off financially if he didn't. The city of Augusta wanted the tournament to return, though, to attract tourism and to be associated with an event that was in turn associated with Jones, so Roberts agreed to revive the Masters.

The first postwar tournament was held in 1946. Ben Hogan had a chance to make up for his playoff loss to Byron Nelson in the last Masters, in 1942, but from twelve feet he three-putted the seventy-second hole and finished a stroke behind the lead. The winner was Herman Keiser, with a 282 total score.

Over the next three years, a couple of familiar names took the title. Jimmy Demaret carded a 281 to win his second Masters in 1947, and in 1949 Sam Snead, shooting consecutive 67s on Saturday and Sunday, became a first-time winner. In between was Claude Harmon, a popular club pro whose sons would become well-known teaching professionals. His 279 total in 1948 tied with the lowest Masters record established by Ralph Guldahl in 1939.

A sad note about the 1948 Masters was that it turned out to be the final competitive appearance of Bobby Jones. He had never come close to winning the tournament, but he hadn't embarrassed himself either. In 1948, however, he did come close to the latter. His score was 315 for seventy-two holes, his worst ever, and he had a 79 in the last round. At forty-six, he was done as a player. (Similar sentiments would be expressed almost forty years later at Augusta National about another great forty-six-year-old golfer.)

Demaret, whose clothing was as colorful as his lifestyle, was almost forty and also fading as a player, but he had enough left for one last Masters victory, in 1950. Snead once said about Demaret having somehow won three Masters, "Not only did Jimmy never practice, I don't think he ever slept." The third championship was a fine cap to a career that had begun in 1935, when he drove out of Houston with six hundred dollars and a set of clubs. Playing pool, he lost the car, then the clubs, then the six hundred dollars. His brother got his clubs out of hock at a pawnshop, and Demaret started earning money as a professional golfer; he won his first tournament three years later.

The next four years had the same two players exchanging jackets. Hogan finally broke through in 1951, his second win in a major since that devastating car crash that almost killed him in 1949. It has been reported routinely over the years that Hogan's stunning and courageous triumph in the 1950 U.S. Open at Merion Golf Club outside Philadelphia (in a playoff over Lloyd Mangrum and George Fazio) was his return to golf after the accident in Texas, but in fact he had played in the Masters that April, his courage awing his fellow competitors.

In 1952 it was Snead's turn, even though his 286 was the highest winning score in the eighteen years since the first Masters. The West Virginian attributed the inflated score to the greens being "slicker'n the top of my head." Dan Jenkins, then a young reporter from Texas, observed that after Hogan helped Snead slip on his second green jacket, the new champion said, "This one don't fit either, but I'll keep it."

Hogan collected his second Masters title in 1953 at the beginning of his "triple slam" season, and in a 180-degree turn from Snead's results the previous year, he set a new low-scoring record, by five strokes, with a 274. At the 1954 Masters, Snead earned his third green jacket in six years by beating—

who else?—Hogan in an eighteen-hole playoff, 70 to the Hawk's 71. Hogan had come within a whisker of winning the fourth major in a row that he had entered, which would not be accomplished by any player until the so-called Tiger Slam of 2000–2001.

Aside from the duel between Snead and Hogan, what caused the most buzz in the 1954 Masters was the play of amateur William Joseph Patton, a twenty-eight-year-old lumber salesman from North Carolina whom everyone called Billy Joe. His loftiest achievement to date had been being appointed as an alternate for the previous year's Walker Cup team. But during a practice round on Wednesday, the good-natured man with a big swing launched a drive of 338 yards, which caught the spectators' attention. That he played well enough through thirty-six holes to easily make the cut had reporters speculating that he could actually contend for the championship through the weekend. He enjoyed whistling between shots, and his drawling comments had fans marveling at his equanimity.

With a 70 on Thursday, Patton was tied for the lead, and he did it on a cold, blustery day that had veteran players tabulating bloated scores. He shot a 74 on Friday, but because the weather was even worse, with rain adding to players' woes, that was actually good enough for sole possession of the lead. The amateur's surprising and seemingly effortless performance—as well as personality—made some of the pros grouchy. Cary Middlecoff was heard to say, "If this guy wins the Masters, it will set golf back fifty years."

For the third round, Patton was paired with Hogan. No problem— Billy Joe just went about his business, outdriving the Hawk and trying not to laugh when his buddies from North Carolina kidded about his partner being "a little guy in a funny white cap." But Hogan had the last laugh, scoring a 69 while Patton fell back down to earth with a 75. In the fourth round, everyone was surprised when the amateur didn't fold. Indeed, by the end of the front nine, which included an ace at 6, Patton had tied Hogan for the lead. But a double bogey on 13 and a bogey at 15 ended his crowd-pleasing run at a Masters title.

With Nelson mostly retired to his ranch in Texas and Hogan and Snead getting long in the tooth, the 1954 Masters was the last major won by a member of the triumvirate that had dominated the most important tournaments in America for over fifteen years. As Jenkins wrote after that marathon Masters playoff finish, "Maybe a golden era was over. Both men are in their forties, and it's doubtful they will ever collide again, head to head, in a duel for a major championship."

This left the door open to others. At the 1955 Masters, Cary Middlecoff shot 279, including a 65 in the second round, earning the victory. (His playing partner in the final round was Byron Nelson; it was the sixth time that Nelson partnered the last eighteen holes with the eventual winner.) Also in 1955, there was an addition at Augusta National in 1955 when the Sarazen Bridge, which runs along one side of the pond in front of the fifteenth green, was dedicated.

In 1956 Jack Burke shot a 289 yet still managed to outlast the field. Ken Venturi had led after three rounds and was still leading at the sixteenth hole, vying to become the first amateur since Johnny Goodman to win a major, but the wheels came off on 17 and 18 when his inexperience with high winds showed. The following year Doug Ford, with a closing round of 66, was fitted for a green jacket. Also in 1957, for the first time at Augusta National, there was a cut after thirty-six holes. This had become necessary because the Tournament Committee had invited an unprecedented 103 participants.

To the players and many golf fans, the Masters had become a unique event, and every player hoped to receive an invitation. "The whole thing here is something you kind of dream about, and when you come here and play, and win this tournament, then it becomes a part of your life," said Byron Nelson. "You look forward to it each year and, of course, the years here have been very good to me."

"When I think of Augusta, I think of great beauty," Gary Player said. "I've always said if they have a golf course like this in heaven, I hope I'm the golf pro there one day."

Raymond Floyd, who hails from North Carolina, recalls, "I grew up about 150 miles from Augusta, Georgia. My little mind game when I was a youngster was, *If I can make par on this hole, I win the Masters; if I can make this putt, I can win the Masters; if I can par the last nine holes, I'll win the Masters. . . .* That was the first tournament I ever remember. I think it's the first time I ever saw televised golf. So, my goal as a kid, of course, was to be a professional golfer and win the Masters."

The Masters was increasing in stature as a national sports event. But there has been some debate as to when it became a major tournament, taking its place alongside the U.S. and British Opens and the PGA Championship.

The latter tournament's star rose as the Western Open's fell. First contested in 1899, the Western Open was the second-oldest tournament in the United States and was third in tenure in North America after the U.S. Open and the Canadian Open. In its earlier years it had attracted a field of players almost as strong, if not as strong, as the U.S. Open, and thus the Western Open was a very important tournament to the players, but that did not translate into it being considered a major in the eyes of the press and national golf officials. As the Professional Golfers' Association increased its membership, its championship event rose to major status, though considered the third among equals.

A change that benefited the Masters was that the U.S. and British Amateur Championships were downgraded from the majors. This became inevitable as more players followed Hagen's lead than Jones's and turned professional, and that meant fewer top-notch golfers competed in the amateur events. Goodman was (and remains) the last amateur to win the U.S. Open, and very few fans were as excited at that as they had been about Jones's wins. Hence, every year after Jones's retirement the general public's interest in the two most well-known amateur events waned.

Because there had been four majors through 1930, it made a kind of sense that there would still be four. With the PGA Championship the third (though only grudgingly accepted by some golf fans and writers), what could be the modern fourth?

Some members of the golf press thought of the Masters as a major right from the beginning, because of its affiliation with Jones. Certainly the influential Grantland Rice wanted readers to think that. Helping his cause was Sarazen's double eagle on 15 in the final round of the 1935 tournament. It generated the most golf headlines since the Jones Grand Slam five years earlier, and it happened at Jones's own club. However, since the tournament was only two years old in 1935, it was a stretch to call it a major so soon.

The overtime duel between Ben Hogan and Byron Nelson in 1942 might have elevated the Masters to major status. But Hogan had not yet achieved the wins or high profile that Nelson and Snead had, and in any case, any major momentum that the tournament had generated came to an immediate halt when Augusta National shut down during the war.

More so than any one event or tournament, it was a combination of factors that turned the Masters into a major championship in the 1950s. One was the trading of green jackets during a four-year run of Snead and Hogan, who by the early years of that decade were the most successful and popular golfers in the world. Hogan even received the Hollywood treatment with the 1951 release of *Follow the Sun*, a biopic starring Glenn Ford and Anne Baxter. It depicts Hogan's early frustrations at trying to break through as a major winner, the head-on collision with the bus, his pain-filled recuperation, and his thrilling victory in the 1950 U.S. Open.

The tournament's affiliation with Bobby Jones continued to be significant. In 1949, he was diagnosed with syringomyelia, a painful and debilitating spinal disease. It would prevent him from playing even friendly practice rounds, and within a few years the disease would put him in a wheelchair. However, though no longer competing on the course, Jones was at Augusta National for every Masters. That the players and many fans could enjoy the presence of golf royalty made the Masters that much more important.

And there was the course. At Augusta National, both practical and aesthetic annual improvements were not the exception but the rule, especially after the club's finances became more stable. As a result, the Masters was played year after year on what was now regarded as one of the best golf venues in the country.

However, it can be argued that what contributed the most to the Masters becoming one of the four international major tournaments were the innovations in how the tournament was conducted that were instituted and overseen by Jones and especially Clifford Roberts. These innovations quickly grew into traditions that resonated all year long among the players and spectators—whom Roberts always referred to as "patrons"—and made the Masters the hottest invitation and ticket in golf.

The green-jacket tradition that had begun in 1949 was unique; in none of the other majors was a distinctive clothing item bestowed upon the winner. The popular Sam Snead was the first player awarded the jacket, and the first ceremony was widely reported. The jackets themselves were first issued to Augusta National Golf Club members in 1937. They were produced by the Brooks Uniform Company in New York City, and Roberts urged the members to wear them during the Masters "with the thought that patrons would thereby be able to identify a reliable source of information." Since 1968, the blazers have been made by Hamilton Tailoring Company of Cincinnati, Ohio.

Long drive, two-man best ball, and other pretournament contests involving many of the well-known players were also unique, as was the personal invitation to participate in the Masters issued by Roberts as tournament chairman. The first pairing sheet could be found at Augusta National, and in 1941 a map of the course had been added to the back of the sheet. In addition, the Masters was the first of the four modern majors to feature seventy-two holes of stroke play spread over four days. For much of its history the U.S. Open had been a three-day event with a thirty-six-hole final round, and it was not until 1958 that the PGA Championship converted to stroke play at all.

Roberts pioneered the use of scoreboards so that the spectators as well as the players knew where each golfer stood. The concession stands were green so they blended in with the trees, and Roberts insisted that what they offered, including pimento sandwiches, be priced affordably for families. Another innovation was introduced in 1960—the "over and under" method of reporting scores: on both scoreboards and the standards carried with each group of golfers, over-par scores were shown in red numerals and under-par scores in green numerals. That same year, a central scoring control room was created. Scores were reported there by phone, and the "controllers" relayed the information so it could be posted on the official scoreboard and passed along to the press building.

The press building had been constructed along the course in 1953 to accommodate newspaper and magazine writers, photographers, radio commentators—and the much-anticipated television sportscasters. For a man born in the 1890s, Roberts had a keen modern eye for the promise of the television medium; he worked to get the Masters on the cutting edge of the technology that would transform the sport. Even before World War II, platforms and small towers for cameramen had been erected, and thus the course was ready for the TV cameras when they began arriving.

The first golf tournament to be televised was the 1947 U.S. Open at the St. Louis Country Club; a local television station covered play at the last hole. (Lew Worsham and Sam Snead finished in a tie; the next day's eighteen-hole playoff, won by Worsham, was not televised.) In 1954 NBC covered the seventeenth and eighteenth holes at Baltusrol for the U.S. Open. Roberts was eager for the Masters to be broadcast as well, but there were no takers among the networks. Finally, CBS tossed him a bone by broadcasting live a total of two and a half hours of the 1956 Masters.

The coverage of the 1956 Masters was much more successful than the previous efforts at the U.S. Open. CBS estimated that ten million viewers watched the tournament. According to Stephen Goodwin in *The Greatest Masters*, "After 1956, when the Masters was first televised, everyone—every American, at least—who followed top-level golf came to know Augusta National as well as or better than any other tournament course in the world. It was every bit as beautiful as the writers had claimed, and people who had never set foot on it knew the key holes by heart. St. Andrews, in Scotland, would always be the most hallowed of courses, but Augusta National could claim to be its American counterpart." Two years later, American Express agreed to sponsor Masters coverage, and everyone involved began making money. With the Masters leading the way, golf was about to grow bigger in popularity thanks to the small screen.

Roberts spurred CBS on every step of the way. A farsighted suggestion of his was for the network to bury television cables on the course. (A precedent of sorts had been set in 1941, when telephone cables were first buried underground around the course, which allowed for immediate scoring updates.) This was something that could not be done for the other majors because the venues changed every year; doing so at Augusta National saved money for CBS and gave the club the security of knowing the network would remain as a broadcaster at least long enough to recoup its substantial investment. At

Roberts's urging, after 1956 CBS kept increasing its coverage, both in time on the air and in the number of holes broadcast.

One account contends that when the intimidating Roberts visited CBS executives in New York City, they served him tea and Oreos with the inside icing removed. Roberts was widely considered a humorless autocrat who ruled the Augusta National Golf Club. "Nothing funny ever happens at Augusta," said Frank Chirkinian, the man in charge of the CBS coverage of the tournament for over thirty years. "Dogs don't bark and babies don't cry. They wouldn't dare."

But Roberts was also known as a courteous man prone to fits of generosity toward workers at the club and younger golfers. His stern expressions did not indicate that he had a sense of humor, but it peeked out from time to time. The night prior to the Jamboree, an annual tournament just for members held two weeks before the Masters, Roberts secretly had workers lower the water level of the pond near the sixteenth tee by eight inches, build a boardwalk across the pond, and return the water to its previous level. During the Jamboree, after hitting his tee shot at 16, Roberts casually strolled across the pond to demonstrate that he could indeed walk on water.

Another powerful figure also helped raise the stature of the Masters Tournament. Dwight D. Eisenhower was a member of Augusta National and would vacation there, a connection to a sitting president that no other major could claim. The World War II hero had wrapped up his military career by the time he made his first trip to Augusta, in April 1948, for his first vacation since before the war. Eisenhower, who was already passionate about golf, and his wife, Mamie, enjoyed the club, its members, and its surroundings.

"Being a great admirer of the nation's most popular war hero, I expected to like the man," Roberts reported in his book. "However, I do not think any of the members who were present expected to find him possessed of so much charm and happy companionship. Ike wanted to play golf, practice golf, or take golf lessons, all day long. He didn't care what he did in the evening, so long as we got started playing bridge as early as possible. It was golf and bridge with almost no interruptions for eleven days in a row."

Eisenhower and Roberts became good friends, and the future president's prospects were certainly enhanced when the chairman introduced him to

Augusta National's members, most of whom had become wealthy and influential businessmen after the war. Roberts played important roles in fund-raising and other chores in the general's successful presidential runs, and he managed Ike's personal investments, helping to make him a millionaire. It was to Augusta that Eisenhower went after election day in 1952; there, well over two hundred thousand people greeted the president-elect.

In all, Eisenhower made forty-nine visits to Augusta National. Ike's Pond was created as an honor to him, and a tree was named for him as well: the Eisenhower Pine on the seventeenth hole, 210 yards from the tee. Mamie's Cottage, named after the First Lady, near the tenth tee, was where the couple stayed. An office was set aside for Eisenhower above the golf shop. He enjoyed painting while there, and five original Eisenhower paintings were hung at the club.

One of the more interesting stories told about him at Augusta National regarded an event that took place during his post–election day stay. Ike's tee shot on 12 landed on a sandbar near Rae's Creek. Roberts, his playing partner, told the president-elect that he could play the ball off the bar. Eisenhower climbed down and sank up to his knees—what he had stepped into was actually quicksand. Secret Service agents yanked him out before he could sink any farther. (The creek, by the way, was named after a former property owner, John Rae, who died in 1789.)

But not even the president of the United States was as influential a visitor to Augusta National as Arnold Palmer. Palmer and the Masters were made for each other. Palmer may well have been the most handsome and dramatic golfer since Jones, and he handled the celebrity much better. As his star was rising, Roberts urged more and more television coverage of the tournament. Palmer's appearances, and victories, at the event would prove especially appealing to the TV audience, and in the ensuing years Palmer would win more Masters than any other major.

He had won the U.S. Amateur Championship in 1954, and in 1955 he played in the Masters for the first time, as the reigning Amateur champion. "I remember like it was yesterday the feeling as I drove up Magnolia Lane into Augusta National Golf Club for the first time," Palmer recalled in his autobiography, *A Golfer's Life*. "I'd never seen a place that looked so beautiful, so well manicured, and so purely devoted to golf, as beautiful as an antebellum estate, as quiet as a church. I remember turning to Winnie [his wife], who was as excited as I was by the sight of the place, and saying quietly, probably as much in awe as I've ever been, 'This has got to be it, Babe.'" His 293 earned him a tie for tenth, an invitation to next year's Masters, and a $696 paycheck.

He turned professional that same year, and captured the Canadian Open. He had eight tour victories by the time he returned to Augusta for the 1958 Masters. His man on the bag was Nathaniel "Ironman" Avery—one of a number of colorfully named African American caddies at the club (Eisenhower's regular caddie was nicknamed Cemetery). After a dramatic birdie on the seventy-second hole, Palmer was the winner by a single stroke. It was Palmer's first major victory, and it added to the perception that he was the most exciting golfer in the world. Palmer was dashing and decisive and held a special appeal for women, who liked his rakish good looks. Even the hungry way he inhaled his cigarettes on the course was thrilling.

That year's tournament offered another opportunity to honor two of the best golfers ever. Just before it began, the Hogan Bridge at the twelfth hole was dedicated. During the same day, a similar ceremony was held for the Nelson Bridge at the thirteenth tee. And North Carolina amateur Billy Joe Patton was still entertaining the patrons. On one hole he was delayed on the tee by the twosome ahead of him. He sprawled on the ground and said, "Holler when they get out of the way."

The following year, Palmer was the favorite, and with seven holes to play on Sunday, he was in fact in the lead. But the first of those seven holes was 12, and Arnie put his tee shot into Rae's Creek. The almost-inevitable triple bogey was too much to overcome, and he watched Art Wall birdie five of the final six holes to beat Cary Middlecoff by a stroke to capture the 1959 Masters.

Palmer, however, took home something perhaps bigger than a victory from Augusta National that April—a step toward acquiring legendary status in American sports. Clifford Roberts had invited soldiers from nearby Camp Gordon to be volunteers at the tournament, and in exchange they got the chance to rub shoulders with their favorite golfers. At one point Palmer noticed one of the scoreboard GIs holding a sign that read ARNIE'S ARMY.

Palmer recalled in his autobiography that it "gave me an electric thrill, I can tell you, as I acknowledged the tribute, to think that in just five years' time my fans had grown from a few hometown folks following me around the Country Club of Detroit to a whole *army* politely rooting for me at Augusta." Patrons also found it inspiring and amusing, and so did the television cameramen and announcers.

They could not see that a storm cloud named Jack Nicklaus was about to have a strong effect on Palmer's sunny view of the Masters.

12

After watching Jack Nicklaus win the 1965 Masters, Bobby Jones remarked, "He plays a game with which I am not familiar." Jones was referring to the unique combination of power and precision that Nicklaus possessed. Coming from an era in which it was rare for a player to drive the ball three hundred yards, and especially to do so accurately, Jones's eyes were opened by the young man from Ohio who could do both routinely. And this raw strength he displayed with the driver did not mean he was careless with other shots. Nicklaus had a deft touch with his irons and the putter. So not only could he get the ball to the greens in fewer strokes, but he also finished off the holes with well-read and well-struck putts.

Arnold Palmer was indeed the most popular player to participate in the Masters, but it was Nicklaus who had the greatest impact on that tournament in the 1960s and 1970s. It is safe to say that if he had not come along when he did, Palmer and Gary Player would have won more green jackets, and a couple of other players would have broken through. And because they would have done so in a less-sensational fashion, fewer changes would have been made to the golf course. But because Nicklaus's game was unfamiliar to Jones, Augusta National had to find ways to keep challenging him.

Jack's first Masters appearance was in 1959. "Before the tournament started, I was shooting these low rounds and thinking this course was not too tough," he recalled in *Jack Nicklaus: My Story*. "Then the tournament started. I three-putted eight times in 36 holes, shot 150, and was on my way home."

But it didn't take him that long to earn his first green jacket. In 1960 Nicklaus made the cut for the first time, tying with Billy Joe Patton for thirteenth; both received the Low Amateur award. He made more progress the next year, earning the same award by tying for seventh and finishing only seven shots behind the winner, Gary Player. He made a slight step back in 1962, when he tied for fourteenth. Still, he felt ready to challenge for the championship in 1963, at the tender age of twenty-three.

He did more than challenge. As Alfred Wright reported in *Sports Illustrated*, "Thanks to an early Georgia springtime, the Augusta National golf course was at its pink-and-white loveliest last week, with the azaleas and dogwood gaily blooming. It seemed a most inappropriate place to use a bludgeon, yet that is what big, smart Jack Nicklaus did as he became, at twenty-three, the youngest golfer ever to win the most cherished tournament of them all."

He took command of the tournament on Friday when he recorded a 66. However, it wasn't the cakewalk that some expected to see after that. Nicklaus motored along comfortably on Saturday, but at the turn during Sunday's final round he had shot a 37 and held only a one-stroke lead over the apparently ageless Snead, the 1961 champion, Player, and Tony Lema.

During the afternoon, the standings fluctuated repeatedly—"so rapidly that one might have thought the scoreboards around the course were being operated by the dealer in a five-card monte game," Wright observed. Player birdied the par-5 15, which prompted him to dance on the green. Snead also birdied the fifteenth, though being a month shy of fifty-one years old he felt less inclined to dance. But Player bogeyed 17 and 18, and Snead did the same on 16 and 18, and their hopes were dashed. Lema parred 18 and waited for Nicklaus to wilt under the pressure and make a mess of the last couple of holes.

He didn't. He had birdied 16 and arrived at 18 at two under, two strokes ahead. He two-putted for the victory and rejoiced by tossing his cap in the air. Wright concluded, "It was evident at Augusta that Nicklaus has become as overwhelming and inevitable as nightfall. The very best competitors in golf may seek to avert him, but he is obviously too strong, too determined, too skillful to be sidetracked or delayed."

Another participant in the Masters that year was Horton Smith, winner of the first tournament at Augusta in 1934 and the third two years later. Though only fifty-five years old in 1963, he was in poor health—he would pass away six months later—but he wanted to play one more tournament. Clifford Roberts and the Masters Committee were totally devoted to the rules of golf, but they would make an exception in Smith's case: he was the only player allowed to use an electric cart on the course, and the press applauded their kindness.

The press was not nearly as generous with Jack Nicklaus. Despite his heavy involvement in sports in high school and college, early in his golf career Nicklaus was a portly man, carrying about 205 pounds. (This had been particularly noticeable in the 1962 U.S. Open, when he was dueling the slender yet muscular Arnold Palmer down the stretch. A few of the many fans who supported the popular Palmer thought that personal insults might derail Nicklaus. They didn't, but they were not fun to hear anyway.) Some newspaper accounts leading up to the 1963 Masters referred to Nicklaus as Ohio Fats and Baby Beef. He was the kind of competitor who used such tasteless reportage as motivation to win.

A side note regarding Nicklaus at the 1963 Masters: Observers noticed that during practice rounds, Jack was taking out a small notebook and writing in it. When asked about it, he revealed that it was a yardage book. Two years earlier, when playing with good friend Deane Beman, the journeyman player who years later would become commissioner of the PGA Tour, he saw Beman walking off yardages and making notations. Jack thought this was a good idea and began doing it himself. Obviously, it helped him, and after the reigning U.S. Open champion won at Augusta that year, other players began to carry small notebooks and pencils on the course too.

At the 1964 Masters, the good news was that Nicklaus had jaws dropping with a 67 in the final round. But it was not enough, as he and Dave Marr wound up six shots behind Palmer, who earned his fourth green jacket. Nicklaus was determined that in the next tournament at Augusta National he wouldn't wait so long to make his move.

For most observers, Nicklaus's blistering third round pretty much sewed up the 1965 Masters. "Jack Nicklaus had curtailed the Masters Championship by 24 hours on Saturday when he waddled around the Augusta National Golf Course in 64 strokes, trampling fallen bodies and records with a big grin on his fresh, round face, but he and the other guys showed up yesterday anyway to play out the farce," wrote Ron Green Sr. of the *Charlotte Observer*.

Nicklaus has called the twelfth hole at Augusta National "maybe the most dangerous short par-3 in golf." On Sunday, he found himself on it with an opportunity not just to win the tournament but to break Ben Hogan's 1953 scoring record—or, by not making the right shot, to rob himself of a second Masters victory.

As Nicklaus later reported in *My Most Memorable Shots in the Majors*, he was thinking, "It would tickle me to break the old record for four rounds, but that's secondary to finishing first." Thus, he didn't shoot for the pin but for the fat of the green. His ball landed safely twenty-five feet from the hole. But to further amaze Jones as well as the patrons, Nicklaus made the birdie putt. He went on from 12 to win the Masters by nine, and his 271 surpassed Hogan's record by three strokes.

"I've never played a more enjoyable round of golf in my life than this one today," the twenty-five-year-old winner told reporters. "I felt confident all day that I could hit the shots."

"We couldn't get close enough for him to know we were even in the field," lamented Palmer. "It was no contest."

For Nicklaus, the 1966 Masters was very different from the 1965 event. He had to truly gut this one out. He did not run away and hide in the first three rounds as he had the year before. And in Sunday's action, he was down three strokes with only five holes to play. But Nicklaus made up that deficit to tie Tommy Jacobs and Gay Brewer at 288 and force an extra round on Monday.

"I don't know how I'm still in this tournament," he said after the fourth round. "But I don't intend to blow it again." It was reported that for dinner that night Nicklaus ate three steaks.

Brewer, who had once caddied for Ben Hogan and parked cars at Augusta National, never really got going in the playoff and was not at all happy with a score of 78. Jacobs played much better and carded a 72. Nicklaus shot a two-under 70, a birdie on 11 helping him to move past Jacobs on the back nine. In Butler Cabin, the building at Augusta National where Clifford Roberts and Bobby Jones traditionally greeted the winner and the lowest-scoring amateur before a homey fireplace, Nicklaus was welcomed by a grinning Jones, who had to be pleased that a golfer who idolized him had found such success at his tournament.

It had taken thirty-two years for the Masters to see its first back-to-back champion. Nicklaus, at only twenty-six, had achieved what had been denied to Sarazen, Hogan, Nelson, Snead, and even Palmer with his four green jackets in seven tries at Augusta National. Winning consecutive Masters made it clear to every player and fan that there was no better golfer than Jack Nicklaus.

What didn't happen, though, was the public or even the press warming up to him that much. "Watching Nicklaus play golf is like watching a bulldozer move dirt," Green wrote at the conclusion of the 1966 Masters. "Gary Player, his partner in the Big Three of golf, is emotional, showy, expansive. Arnold Palmer, the other member of the Grand Triumvirate, is animated, a slam-bang gambler who has a mystic communication with his worshipping galleries. Nicklaus is none of these things. He is a nice guy, but he can't seem to get that point across, because he can play golf better than anybody on the planet, and a lot of people seem to resent his particular brand of excellence." Green did allow, "It's a bad rap. It's like pulling against Sandy Koufax simply because he's the best pitcher in baseball."

According to Alfred Wright in *Sports Illustrated*, "There is no reason to think that 26-year-old Jack Nicklaus won't win every Masters Championship from now until the year 2000." Wright and others, as well as Nicklaus himself, would be surprised that no more green jackets would be added to his closet for the rest of the decade and into the next one.

13

Friday of the 1986 edition of the Masters was another bright, windy day, and thus it was expected that balls would roll faster across the drying grass of the greens. It could be the final day at Augusta National for those players who had had a tough time of it on Thursday. One of the foreign young guns, Nick Price, for example, had posted a startling 79, and everyone knew he was much better than that. One way or another, Friday would separate the better golfers from those who didn't have the right stuff, and the former would be joined on the weekend by a few surprises from the rest of the field.

Seve Ballesteros showed up for his second round looking like he meant business—dressed in black and ready to scowl if even a bird chirped at him the wrong way. Because of the contretemps with Beman and the PGA Tour, this Masters was personal. His outfit and demeanor stated that only a victory would restore his honor. Gordon S. White Jr. observed in his *New York Times* account, "Ballesteros seems like a man with a cause this week, as if he is out to show Beman just who is the best."

The Spaniard, however, was tactful: "My determination has always been a part of me."

He parred the first hole. After a huge drive of 360 yards, he birdied the second hole, having reached the green in two. He made another birdie at the par-3 sixth. It was classic Ballesteros on the seventh: drive with a 2-iron, sand wedge onto the green, make the ten-foot uphill putt. Ballesteros wasn't waiting for the weekend to make a strong move.

Other competitors weren't standing there gawking, however. Bernhard Langer shot an even-par 35 on the front nine—not great, but an improvement over Thursday's 74. At the turn, Tom Watson also had a 35, and Greg Norman was one shot better. At four under, he and Ballesteros were tied for the lead.

Bill Kratzert was hanging in. The man with eyeglasses large enough to rival Tom Kite's didn't have the touch he had demonstrated on Thursday, but at least he wasn't going backward. Also staying near the top of the leaderboard were Tommy Nakajima, Danny Edwards, Ben Crenshaw, and T. C. Chen. Kite was struggling. And so was Jack Nicklaus, but not too badly.

The patrons cheered everything he did, because of his five Masters wins and the increasing realization that he would not have many more opportunities to add a sixth. Jack could play at Augusta National for as long as he could walk the course—heck, if it ever came to that, he would probably be allowed to use a cart like Horton Smith did—but everyone knew his competitive fire. If he couldn't play up to his own standards, he would no longer participate in the Masters. At age forty-six, if he followed Thursday's 74 with the same or a worse number and didn't make the cut, this 1986 tournament could even be it for the Golden Bear.

A few patrons had to wonder if the repeated lengthening of the Augusta National course had made it too much of a physical test for an aging Nicklaus to seriously compete for one more championship. This would be ironic, because his early dominance of the tournament and golf in general had prompted the Tournament Committee to expand the yardage. For the 1986 Masters, the course was 6,905 yards. However, a scoring official told the *New York Times* that "the walking length of this course is over 8,000 yards." By the fourth round, or perhaps even the third one—assuming Nicklaus got that far—those forty-six-year-old legs carrying a frame not as lean as in past years could become quite tired.

But his putting improved on Friday—not to a particularly impressive level, but he made most of the ones he had to make on the front-nine holes—while his ball striking remained solid. *Just keep shooting par and make the cut,* was what many patrons were thinking. They knew that wouldn't be enough to satisfy Nicklaus, but it would still be enough.

14

Even with the maturity that Nicklaus had shown in the clutch when he won the U.S. Amateur Championship the year before, he was still only twenty years old when he arrived at Cherry Hills for the 1960 U.S. Open. What an age to be paired in the final round with Ben Hogan, who was threatening, at forty-eight, to win his fifth national championship. That Nicklaus wasn't yet up to Open pressure was displayed on the 385-yard, par-4 thirteenth hole.

He was one stroke ahead of Arnold Palmer, Julius Boros, and Jack Fleck (whose improbable win five years earlier had denied Hogan a fifth Open), and the Hawk was two shots back. Jack's second shot landed twelve feet from the pin. A birdie would probably bury Hogan with five holes left. Too pumped up by that thought, he sent the putt eighteen inches past the hole. Impeding the way back was an indentation left by a poorly repaired ball mark.

"Excited, anxious, under as much pressure as I've even known, I can't focus my mind clearly on whether the rules allow me to repair the ball mark [they do]," Nicklaus wrote in his book *My Most Memorable Shots in the Majors*. "Also, I'm too shy or embarrassed to admit this in front of Hogan or to hold up play by asking an official." He missed the comeback putt, and Palmer came out on top to capture the Open—in a patented charge, he shot a 65 in the final round.

In future tournaments, however, it would be Nicklaus providing the intimidation.

His close call at the Open forced him to make a decision that he had been delaying. Because of his admiration for Bobby Jones, Nicklaus allowed himself to believe that he would remain an amateur. But his play at Cherry Hills against most of the best golfers in the world surely indicated that he could make a living as a professional. Helping to tip the scales was his recent marriage to Barbara Bash, a young woman from Columbus whom he had met at Ohio State. To support a family, he would need to earn more than he was making selling insurance part-time back in Ohio.

Nicklaus didn't cross over to being a professional right away. He had unfinished business. His victory at the 1959 U.S. Amateur had made him the youngest champion in that event in half a century, and he wanted to defend his title. He didn't—not in 1960. In the third round he three-putted six times en route to a defeat that sent him packing.

He remained an amateur in 1961 so he could take another crack at that national championship. But his good showing in the 1961 Masters and his tie for fourth in the U.S. Open, only three shots behind the winner, Gene Littler, was further evidence that he could compete at the highest level. Nicklaus took the NCAA Championship and headed to Pebble Beach in the hopes of becoming the first golfer in history to win that event and the U.S. Amateur in the same year.

Pebble Beach, right on the Pacific Ocean in California and host to five U.S. Opens, the most recent being in 2010, would become Nicklaus's favorite course in the United States (with Augusta National a very close second). From the beginning, he didn't need much convincing. "I am not usually given to snap decisions, but I fell in love with Pebble Beach from the moment I first played it in practice that year," he wrote in *Jack Nicklaus: My Story*. "'Inspired' is a strong word, but that was the effect Pebble Beach had on me as the 1961 U.S. Amateur Championship got under way."

"Inspired" may actually be an understatement considering how Nicklaus performed that week. After a bye in the first round, he played the next 136 holes in twenty-under-par up until the final match. "I enjoyed a week of golfing heaven," he recalled. The finale, against H. Dudley Wysong Jr.

of Texas, whose father had once taken lessons from Byron Nelson, was no exception. After Wysong conceded for the 8 and 6 win, Nicklaus had his second Amateur Championship.

For the third year in a row, he was named the world's top amateur player by *Golf Digest*. He was on the top rung as an amateur, with nowhere higher to go. When 1962 began, Nicklaus was a professional golfer. He was also a father, with Barbara having given birth to Jackie.

Another important off-course happening that year came when the founder of the sports agency IMG, Mark McCormack, who was Arnold Palmer's agent and would later represent Nicklaus too, was interviewed by the *Age* newspaper in Melbourne, Australia. The writer quoted McCormack's description of the "large, strong, and blond" Nicklaus and referred to him in the article as "the Golden Bear." The apt nickname stuck.

Nicklaus played steadily in 1962, though he earned a few dollars here, a few dollars there. He might not necessarily have felt ready for the U.S. Open at Oakmont—Palmer's home turf, as he hailed from Latrobe, Pennsylvania—but like in 1960, he was the reigning U.S. Amateur champion and he had to give it his best shot.

To the delight of fans, it came down to him and Palmer—well, at Oakmont they were almost all delighted about Palmer charging toward another championship. During the first fifty-four holes, the course was an unfriendly and occasionally hostile environment for the twenty-two-year-old from Ohio. Yet he kept grinding. No doubt many others in the field were impressed by Nicklaus's physical gifts (especially as he routinely outdrove them) but believed that the young amateur who didn't look like he even shaved yet would stumble in the final round, especially on the back nine. Instead, one by one, other competitors fell by the wayside, and he and Palmer were tied with two holes left.

On the 292-yard, par-4 seventeenth hole, Nicklaus faced a putt that was as pressure-packed as the one he had flubbed on 13 in the 1960 Open. "There's a tremendous urge to rush very critical short putts, to get them over with, to release the almost unbearable tension," he mused. "Usually, that's fatal. Somehow I force myself to set up very carefully, jiggling around until I'm certain about both my body alignment and the putter face: both dead square to the hole."

He made the four-footer to stay tied with Palmer. He parred 18, and then watched as Palmer failed to birdie 17 and 18 to grab the title. Instead, the tournament went into a playoff. During the press conference, Arnie looked at Jack and said with evident affection, "That big, strong dude—I thought I was through with him yesterday. I'd rather be playing somebody else."

If he had been playing anyone else he would have won his second U.S. Open. But in the playoff, Nicklaus opened a lead on the back nine, and his 71 to Palmer's 74 gave him his first professional major championship.

Palmer was impressed by the decade-younger man's mental strength. Reflecting years later on the 1962 Open, Palmer wrote, "Jack Nicklaus was a different animal altogether, completely unlike anybody I'd ever chased. For one thing, he didn't seem the slightest bit bothered by the electricity of my charge and the lusty cries of my supporters. If anything, they seemed to drive him further into that hard cocoon of concentration he showed the world. But it would take the world years to fully appreciate how difficult a chore that was and how well he executed it. I had never seen anyone who could stay focused the way he did—and I've never seen anyone with the same ability since."

Nicklaus had overcome the taunts and other distractions of Palmer's loyal fans, and his subsequent appearance on the cover of *Time* magazine may not have made him as popular as Palmer, but it obviously enshrined him as the face of a new kind of player. At only twenty-two, he was the youngest winner of the U.S. Open since Bobby Jones, of course, who was twenty-one when he took his first Open in 1923. (No one younger has won that championship since Nicklaus.)

The rest of his first year as a professional was also promising. He won two tournaments on the PGA Tour, tied for third in his debut at the PGA Championship, was named the PGA Rookie of the Year, and with sixty thousand dollars was third on the tour's money list. Jack Nicklaus had arrived. It remained to be seen if he had staying power.

He did. From 1962 through 1970 he won thirty-three PGA tournaments and numerous international contests, and he began to chip away at Walter Hagen's record of eleven professional majors. His earnings surged—he hit the one-hundred-thousand-dollar mark at the end of 1963, and from that year through 1970 he practically lapped the field by collecting over a million dollars in official tour winnings, more than any other player in the 1960s. (Understandably, he left the insurance game behind.) His earnings were easily eclipsed by endorsements and other off-course income, including revenue from the businesses he founded.

But victory in the world's most visible golf events brought him the most joy—outside of his expanding family. Winning the 1962 Open and following that up with three Masters in four years put him on the same level as the older Palmer and Gary Player. For the rest of the decade and into the 1970s, Player continued to earn victories in major championships, and Lee Trevino burst out of Texas to win several, but no one in golf gathered them in batches like Nicklaus did. He truly became the man to beat.

He won his first PGA Championship in 1963, and coupled with the win at Augusta National, this marked the first year that he won two majors, matching what Palmer had done in 1960 when he won both the Masters and U.S. Open. He still had to look up to Palmer, though, because he was second to the King on the 1963 PGA Tour money list. The following year he beat out Palmer by the grand sum of $81.13. In all of 1964, during which he entered thirty-one tournaments, Nicklaus missed just one cut.

In 1965 he didn't miss a single cut. Of twenty-eight tournaments, he won five and came in second seven times. It was no longer news when Nicklaus won but when he *didn't* win. Again he finished the year on top of the money list. The next year he became a two-time major winner again when, after repeating as Masters champion, he earned his first Claret Jug by winning the British Open at Muirfield in Scotland. This triumph also meant that at only twenty-six he was the youngest player in golf history to notch the modern Career Grand Slam; he joined Gene Sarazen, Ben Hogan, and Gary Player in doing so. It was an extremely difficult achievement—the Career Grand Slam eluded such greats as Hagen, Nelson, Snead, and Palmer.

In 1967 Nicklaus won a second U.S. Open, at Baltusrol, his 275 breaking Hogan's record by one shot. Especially impressive was that only he and Palmer, who was second by four shots, broke par for the tournament. Nicklaus was second in the British Open and third in the PGA Championship and was the money leader that year once more, all factors in his being named the PGA Tour Player of the Year.

Only someone with Nicklaus's achievements could be viewed as having a slump the next couple of years. He did not win a major in 1968 or 1969, and the highest he finished on the money list from 1968 through 1970 was second. He won other tournaments around the world, though, including eight on the newly formed PGA Tour during the period.

Two events in 1970 affected him deeply. The first was a sad one, in February, when Charlie Nicklaus died, at only fifty-six. "My father's death was a traumatic experience for me," Jack wrote in *Jack Nicklaus: My Story*. "Ever since I could remember he had been so much more than just a father: My guide, my companion, my mentor, my supporter, my defender, but always most of all my closest and surest friend." He added that Charlie Nicklaus "was the rock I could always turn to whenever the need arose."

The other event took place that July, when he won a second British Open, this time at St. Andrews. The weather was a major obstacle, with winds gusting over fifty miles per hour. After defeating Doug Sanders with a birdie putt on 18—his tee shot with a 3-wood had traveled 380 yards—he threw his putter in the air and was clearly emotionally spent.

For Nicklaus, the decade from his near-win of the U.S. Open as an amateur in 1960 through his marathon victory at St. Andrews rivaled and perhaps exceeded the great decades of Hagen and Jones in the 1920s, Nelson in the 1940s, Hogan in the 1950s, and Palmer's somewhat abbreviated one that lasted from his first Masters victory in 1958 to his final one in 1964. Still only thirty years old in 1970, Nicklaus had earned eight majors, and if he could win one more PGA Championship, he would become the only golfer to win all four majors twice.

Perhaps his only frustration was that since his last victory at Augusta National in 1966, Jack had been unable to match Palmer's four green jackets.

15

By the 1960s, the Masters had acquired a mystique unlike any other tournament. It was a very special event to have a British Open contested at St. Andrews or a U.S. Open at one of the great older courses like Oakmont and Oakland Hills, but for the best players it was a distinct honor to be invited to Augusta National every April. It was special for the fans who followed the tournament, too.

"This feeling of extraordinary kinship with the Masters is not restricted to those who go to Augusta," wrote Herbert Warren Wind in a 1962 essay for the *New Yorker*. "In general, golf fans celebrate and talk about their preoccupation as no other sports group does, and the talk of the returning pilgrims about the Masters—abetted to some degree by the telecasts and by the year-round rhapsodies of the golf-writing press—has created such an inordinate wave of interest in the event that many men who have never set foot on the course have acquired a knowledge of it that really is amazing."

Wind was already citing television as a factor in the tournament's growing popularity, and Arnold Palmer was already leading the charge in drawing TV audiences to the event. Of course, to do so most effectively, Palmer had to remain in contention on Sunday—or, even better, to win. He'd failed to do so in the 1959 Masters, but he was back in 1960 seeking his second major. It was already a good year, with four victories including the ninety-hole Palm Springs Golf Classic (later known as the Bob Hope Desert Classic). His forward momentum continued at Augusta National: he opened with a 67, the lowest round for anyone in the tournament, and his lead persisted through the Friday and Saturday rounds. Yet with three holes to play on Sunday, he was overtaken by Ken Venturi. "Mr. Palmer, are we choking?" his caddie asked.

Not to worry: with a thirty-foot birdie putt on 17 and a six-foot birdie on 18, Palmer earned a one-stroke triumph. "Nothing else in the world mattered as Palmer studied his putt, stepped over it and tapped it toward the left corner of the hole," reported Ron Green Sr., who covered the Masters for forty-five years. "It rolled lazily, turned slowly to the right, and dropped in, and the quiet Augusta countryside exploded with the thunder of the thrilled thousands." His ecstatic leap into the air on the eighteenth green was a perfect TV moment.

The following year, with the 1960 U.S. Open victory to his name, Palmer aimed to become the first back-to-back Masters champion. But that was the year that Gary Player broke through, scoring 280 to capture the trophy. Arnie had putting problems but recovered "and 'charged,'" he remembered. "I came to the final tee three under for the day, holding a one-stroke lead, needing just par to become the first man in history to win consecutive Masters Championships"—five years ahead of Jack Nicklaus. But, Palmer lamented, "I simply blew it": he double-bogeyed 18 and lost to Player by a stroke.

By April 1962, Palmer had added the British Open to his collection of majors, but back at Augusta, he had some trouble in the final round. According to Green, "Even the most unreasonable Palmer idolaters must have doubted his chances of retrieving a piece of first place when he hit his tee shot over the green at the watery, par-3 16th. He trailed [Dow] Finsterwald by three shots and Player by two at that point, but—only the Good Lord knows how or why—he chipped in from fifty feet for a birdie two. The roar that went up from the green valley must have been heard in Valdosta." Palmer again thrilled TV viewers and his growing army by sinking a twenty-footer for birdie at 17. He shot a bloated 75 for the round, but his total of 280 was enough to send him into a playoff with Player and Finsterwald.

In the playoff, his 68 easily trumped Player's 71 and Finsterwald's 77. Palmer went on to win a total of eight times in 1962, including his second British Open.

As Hogan and Snead had done in the 1950s at Augusta National, Palmer and Nicklaus did in the 1960s. After helping Nicklaus into the green jacket in 1963, Palmer was more determined than ever to win the Masters for a fourth time the following year. He did, and his 276 total was the lowest since Hogan's in 1953. It would turn out to be his last Masters victory, though he was only thirty-three at the time.

In the final round of the 1964 tournament, he was paired with Dave Marr, who would win a PGA Championship in 1965 and captain the powerful 1981 U.S. Ryder Cup team. Palmer's lead was six strokes as the duo approached the eighteenth tee. Since Marr was tied for second place with Nicklaus, and Palmer knew that beating out the defending champion for second would be huge for Marr, the leader asked him if he could do anything to help. Marr replied, "Sure, Arnold, you could take a 12."

Elsewhere at the 1964 Masters, a club pro was having an especially good week. Davis Love Jr. shot a 69 in the opening round, tying for the lead. The twenty-nine-year-old shot a 75 on Friday but still made the cut. He didn't threaten first place for the remainder of the tournament, but he was still smiling a few days later when his wife gave birth to Davis Love III.

After Nicklaus became the first back-to-back winner in 1965 and 1966, he and Palmer allowed a few other players to earn green jackets. Gay Brewer won in 1967. Also that year, the BBC carried a live telecast of the Masters via satellite to its viewers in Great Britain. It was the first live showing of a golf tournament to an overseas audience.

Ben Hogan's tenth-place finish in 1967 would be the last competitive round at Augusta National for the two-time Masters champion. He knew it was time to hang up his clubs there. The 1967 event was the seventeenth time he had finished in the top ten in the twenty-five Masters Tournaments he played in, and at age fifty-five it was unlikely he would add to that achievement.

The following year Bob Goalby was the surprise winner when forty-five-year-old Roberto De Vicenzo signed the incorrect scorecard. (The fact that

Goalby shot an excellent 66 in the last round, the kind of thing winners do under pressure, is often overlooked.) Also remarkable about the 1968 Masters was Arnold Palmer's failure to make the cut.

The decade ended with George Archer becoming champion. More significantly, there was no more blackout of the tournament on local TV. When the Masters was first televised in 1956, CBS was required to black out its coverage within a two-hundred-mile radius of Augusta National, to help boost ticket sales. Thirteen years later, such boosting was no longer necessary, and the last remnant of the blackout was lifted.

Bobby Jones was not on the course to watch the action at the 1969 Masters. He was too ill, but he managed to watch the TV coverage in his cabin near the tenth tee. Somehow, the great amateur golfer endured the incessant pain his spine disease caused, but over the next two years he would receive fewer and fewer visitors.

Walter Hagen was the first of his great triumvirate to die, in 1969 at the age of seventy-six. It was Jones's turn on December 18, 1971, when the physical agony that he had stoically endured finally ended. (Gene Sarazen would live until 1999, passing away at ninety-seven.) Jones's death made headlines around the world, and the Augusta National Golf Club went into deep mourning. Not an emotionally demonstrative man, Roberts, who had remained one of Jones's closest friends for over forty years, wrote in his book, "I am the one who proposed the idea of making Bob President in Perpetuity [of Augusta National]. I was also the coauthor, along with James M. Hull, of the resolution that did so. In view of this, and my many expressions in these passages of high regard and affection for Bob Jones, I shall not try to describe my sense of personal loss. Any such effort, I feel, would be redundant."

According to Herbert Warren Wind, in an essay that he began to write at Augusta National several months after Jones's death: "This April everyone felt his absence sharply and continually. I think this was to be expected. What was surprising was the sense of shock and grief that so many people in golf experienced when word came of his death. After all, we had been prepared for this news for years, and, in addition, in a corner of our hearts we knew it would be a blessing. . . . And yet, how hard the news hit when it came! In another corner of our hearts we had been nursing the faint hope that somehow or other Jones would make it back to Augusta one of these springs and we would be seeing him again and talking with him again, and now we knew we wouldn't."

At the 1970 Masters, in what would turn out to be the last eighteen-hole playoff at Augusta National, Billy Casper shot 69 to Gene Littler's 74 to secure the green jacket. At thirty-eight, Casper had earned forty-four PGA Tour titles and had won the U.S. Open in 1959 and 1966. Indeed, his twenty-seven victories between 1964 and 1970 were more than Palmer, Nicklaus, and Player won during the same period. He was a stud on the Ryder Cup teams: his total of 22 points in the event remains the most of any American player. Yet because of his quiet nature (and not having Palmer's TV-friendly looks), he was not as popular with the public. His fellow players knew how good he was, though, and no one begrudged him his only Masters victory.

One of the most peculiar events in a Masters occurred in the 1970 edition. During the midafternoon, a rumor circled the club that while on the thirteenth hole, Palmer had suffered a heart attack. This wasn't true, but he was already three over par and no doubt felt sick enough about that.

There were two repeat winners during the decade. One of them was Jack Nicklaus, in 1972 and 1975. Gary Player earned his second jacket in 1974, which was kind of a comeback, because in the previous year he had won only one tournament and had endured two serious surgeries. Indicating his satisfaction, after Player finished off the seventy-second hole he told Dave Stockton, his playing partner, "I deserved to win. I played the best I've ever played from tee to green." Forty years after the first Masters, Player remained the only foreigner to win the championship.

On the flip side of the coin, a fine player, Tom Weiskopf, finished second three times in the 1970s, and with his runner-up finish in 1969 he was a bridesmaid at Augusta National four times in seven years. Weiskopf never did win a Masters, but he gained some consolation from winning the British Open in 1973.

Oddly, one of the best American players never to win a Masters was Lee Trevino. The Mexican American from Texas had broken through in 1968 by winning the U.S. Open at Oak Hill in Rochester, shooting four rounds under

70—the first player to do so in an Open—and defeating Nicklaus by four shots. (By carding a 68 in his final round, fifty-six-year-old Sam Snead tied for ninth, his last finish in the top ten in the Open.) Because of this victory, Trevino was invited to Augusta the following April.

"Through the years a lot of people have thought I hate the Masters, the city, the people and everything else in Augusta," wrote Trevino in his auto-biography, *They Call Me Super Mex*. "That's not true. Actually, I really liked the Masters when I was first invited to play."

However, he rarely performed well in the tournament. Even though he shot a 69 in the final round of his first Masters (after learning that morning that his son Tony had been born), the following week at the Tournament of Champions he complained in the locker room to another player that he didn't like Augusta National and might well not play there again. He was overheard by Bob Green, an Associated Press reporter, who published the comments.

Clifford Roberts took the high road by continuing to invite Trevino, who refused the invitations in 1970 and 1971. He was back in 1972 at the urging of Nicklaus, but he almost packed up and left during his first practice round when, because of a misunderstanding about proper badges, a police officer tried to remove his caddie from the course. Out of respect for Nicklaus and the event, Trevino continued to play the Masters when he was invited, but he never felt confident enough to win there.

He would later write, "If I never win the Masters, it will be my fault. If I'd had a different outlook, I think I could have already won there." Unfortunately, a player who won two U.S. Opens, two British Opens, and two PGA Championships (the last in 1984 at age forty-four) never came close to completing a Career Grand Slam.

In 1971 Charles Coody won his green jacket, beating runners-up Nicklaus and Johnny Miller. After Nicklaus's 1972 victory, Tommy Aaron was fitted for one in 1973. (One can surmise that he thoroughly checked his scorecard after playing a part in the gaffe that cost De Vicenzo the Masters title five years earlier.)

After Nicklaus's fifth victory in 1975 came back-to-back wins by players who had won majors elsewhere: Raymond Floyd with a record-breaking 271 and eight-stroke victory in 1976 (he had won the PGA Championship in

1969), and Tom Watson in 1977 (two years after he won the British Open). And Fuzzy Zoeller became the first of the new under-thirty generation to become a Masters champion, in that three-way playoff in 1979.

There was a sad note to the 1976 Masters. The day before the first round, Clifford Roberts announced that he was retiring as Masters chairman, at eighty-two. His bouts of ill health wouldn't allow him to continue, and William Lane, a Houston businessman, became only the second chairman of the tournament in forty-three years. Even those who weren't particularly fond of Roberts had to acknowledge that as much as Bobby Jones—and many would argue more so—he was responsible for the Masters becoming a unique major tournament.

Two years earlier, when Roberts turned eighty, a birthday party had been thrown for him at Augusta National. During the dinner, rather than talk about himself and his forty-plus years of accomplishments at the club, his talk was devoted to four African Americans who had worked at the club for four decades. Among them was Robert Reynolds, ninety-one, who had actually helped to construct the course before there was an Augusta National Golf Club.

It was a time of endings, but also of welcome returns. Ben Hogan hadn't set foot on the grounds of Augusta National since leaving after his last round in 1967, but he was back at the club, finally, in 1978. As a past Masters champion he could have played, but at sixty-six he knew it would be a painful experience. He came back to attend his first Champions Dinner since his departure. He told the other champions he'd had a dream that he made seventeen straight birdies, but after only parring 18 he woke up angry.

By 1978, many believed that Gary Player's years as a winner—certainly as a major champion—were also well behind him. At forty-two, he had not won a tournament in the United States in four years. But that year, the globe-trotting South African turned back the clock. He strung three strong rounds together, and his 30 on the back nine on Sunday was a thing of beauty. But his 277 total might well not have held up, considering that three men were still out on the course who could snatch the title away from Player.

Rod Funseth might not have struck fear into any competitor's heart, especially since he was three years older than Player, but Hubert Green was the reigning U.S. Open champion and Tom Watson was the defending Masters champion. Watson, in particular, was fourteen years younger than Player and moving into his peak years. But he bogeyed 18, Funseth's par left him a stroke short, and Green had a putt of less than three feet to force a playoff. That turned out to be too far to go.

"After Green missed his critical putt, it was almost as if reality were suspended for a moment, like motion-picture film jamming in a projector," reported Herbert Warren Wind. "Everyone at the eighteenth had been thinking only of hurrying to the first hole for the playoff. It seemed like ages before Green walked over and made the tap-in that didn't count. While he did this, the gallery remained transfixed. Then it slowly dawned on the vast assembly that what they had seen had actually occurred: The tournament was over, and Gary Player had won it." It was Player's ninth and final major. And anticipating what would happen in a few years to another ancient mariner of golf courses, it was Player's most satisfying.

After Clifford Roberts stepped down as chairman, he continued to spend much of his time at Augusta National, when he was not at the home of his third wife in Beverly Hills. But his health was failing. He recovered from a mild stroke but was in a weakened condition. In early spring 1977, he spent a week in St. Luke's Episcopal Hospital in Houston. He was back in Augusta when the Masters began but was not well enough to be out on the course.

He returned to St. Luke's in September, because he was losing weight and feeling more fatigued. He was diagnosed with dementia, though another doctor disputed it. In any case, Roberts knew that his condition was not going to improve and only pain and indignity lay ahead. Unlike Jones, he was not going to stick it out.

He was flown back to Augusta National. According to *The Making of the Masters* by David Owen, on his last day at the club, Roberts got his hair cut, had a receptionist buy him a pair of pajamas, consumed his usual late-afternoon tea and pound cake, and asked a waiter, Ray Wigfall, to help him out to the first tee. He spent a long time gazing out at the course. That night, he ate alone in his room, called his wife, and until ten o'clock chatted with Wigfall.

Some time after Wigfall left, Roberts put trousers on over his pajama pants and put his slippers on the wrong feet. On the envelope containing his medical chart from St. Luke's he wrote a note to his wife: "Dear Betty: I am sorry. I love you. Cliff." His body was found the next morning.

Roberts had apparently wandered out onto the golf course, to the lower end of Ike's Pond near the par-3 course. There he shot himself in the temple—taking his own life just as his mother had some sixty years before.

In the final paragraph of his book on Augusta National, Roberts wrote about the place that was truly his home: "I would like in conclusion to make the observation that those with talent who give unselfishly of themselves just because they love golf are entitled to one uncomplicated place where they can feel completely at ease."

Because he loved golf so dearly, Roberts probably would have welcomed the sea change that took place in the sport just a few years after his death—and the excitement, challenge, and fine play that it produced. In 1980 the foreign invasion of major tournaments on U.S. soil began in the most sustained way. The beachhead was Augusta.

16

Augusta National didn't cooperate with Nicklaus's desire to win the Masters every year. While he was building the best resume in golf and winning other major championships, after 1966 green jackets were hard to come by.

It was an especially rude return to reality in the 1967 Masters when his 79 in the second round—the worst number he would ever post at Augusta National—made him miss the cut for the first time since 1959. He played much better in 1968 but still only tied for fourth, four strokes behind Bob Goalby. He finished ten shots behind George Archer and tied for twenty-eighth the following year.

A new decade didn't offer a turning point. Nicklaus was barely on the radar screen in the 1970 tournament won by Billy Casper. In 1971 a 68 in the third round had him tied with Charles Coody. But that twelfth hole got involved, and he finished tied with Johnny Miller for second, two shots behind Coody.

Nicklaus finally had a reason to smile in 1972—he was running away with the Masters Tournament. But maybe he was like someone leaping off a cliff who realizes he truly can't fly: he staggered a bit in the final round. As Dan Jenkins explained in *Sports Illustrated*, Nicklaus might have been think-ing about the Masters scoring record, because "that's what made Nicklaus come limping down the stretch over those last few holes, trying to play it cozy, trying not to let the Masters slip away to some guy who didn't want it in the first place. He went to the eleventh hole of the last round with a five-stroke lead on the pack, which included somebody named Jim Jamieson, and *he* was supposed to get you excited? You've got to be drunker than most everybody under the umbrellas on the veranda."

Perhaps the best thing to happen to Nicklaus on the back nine of the final round was his performance on the twelfth hole. The wind was making the course even dryer than before, and the par-3 was almost unplayable. His 3-iron tee shot landed ten feet short of the stick, but because the green was like glass, the ball went through the green and down the steep bank behind it.

His tricky pitch was a disappointment, with the ball left in the rough at the top of the bank. He popped the ball onto the green, but again it traveled too fast and came to rest eight feet past the cup. "Now I'm in real danger of giving it all away," he thought—referring not just to the Masters but his determination to go for the modern Grand Slam.

He tapped the ball gently, and it rolled in for a bogey. That shot, Nicklaus later told reporters, reenergized him and helped to sharpen his usual laser-like focus in the final round of a major.

He finished with 286. That was only two under par but enough to win by three strokes, with three players—Jamieson being one—tied at 289. With the greens being especially tough, Nicklaus was the only player under par.

"I figured I had them if I didn't make any dumb mistakes," he said afterward, about keeping the ball dry on 12. "If someone had started to move up on me, I think I could have turned it on a little, because I was hitting the ball better than I had all week. If I had been pressed, I would have taken different tactics and probably wouldn't have made as many bogeys."

Jack wasn't boasting; he was just being his usual blunt self. Still, it was probably salt in the wound for Arnold Palmer, who shot an 81 in the final round and accumulated 300 strokes during the tournament.

There would be no consecutive championships at Augusta National this time around. In the 1973 tournament, he tied for third with Peter Oosterhuis and the still-surprising Jamieson, one stroke behind J. C. Snead (a nephew of

Sam) and two behind the winner, Tommy Aaron. And 1974 saw the come-back Masters championship of longtime rival Gary Player.

Another Nicklaus rival was in contention after the first two rounds of the 1975 Masters: Arnold Palmer. At forty-five, he shot 69 and 71 on Thursday and Friday to put him in a tie for second place. It was like old times at Augusta National.

Said his playing partner Tom Watson, all of twenty-five, "They cheer louder for him here than anywhere else. I've never heard cheers like that. Ten million decibels. I can understand why. He's the man who made our game what it is."

Palmer faded over the weekend, but there were other big names in contention to satisfy patrons, especially when several of them duked it out for the green jacket. Johnny Miller shot a 65 and 66, Tom Weiskopf a 66 and 70. Nicklaus needed all of the six-stroke and eleven-stroke leads he had on Weiskopf and Miller after thirty-six holes thanks to his 68 and 67 on Thursday and Friday.

The slugfest came down to the end of the final round. With Weiskopf and Miller sculpting their excellent back nines, Nicklaus birdied 15. On the par-3 sixteenth hole, his 5-iron tee shot landed left and forty feet short of the hole. To add to his predicament, from where he stood on the green he could see both Weiskopf and Miller birdie the fifteenth, putting them one ahead and one behind him, respectively.

Nicklaus gazed intently at the putt of Watson, his playing partner during the last eighteen holes, and saw it curve to the left sharply after cresting the hill. He envisioned that line in his mind as he stood over his own putt. Jack, wearing distinctive white pants and shoes and a green-and-white-striped shirt, struck the ball, it followed his vision, and while it was still twelve feet from the hole he knew it was in. He lifted the putter high over his head. And as the ball dropped in for birdie, both he and his caddie, Willie Peterson, leaped into the air. Then Nicklaus ran around the green, allowing Tom Weiskopf to say that he left "bear tracks." The crowd roared, rattling his two rivals as Jack took the lead. Prior to the 1986 Masters, many fans considered this display to be the most famous Nicklaus moment at a major.

As each year passed, more fans and members of the media came to believe that Jack Nicklaus had won his final Masters in 1975. Speculation was rife that Jack was ready to pass his crown to such hot players as Lee Trevino, Tom Watson, and Johnny Miller. And with the great finish the '75 tournament provided, there should have been no regrets.

17

While the Masters drought appeared to be permanent, Nicklaus was far from finished as a winner of major golf tournaments. During the 1970s, the Golden Bear was actually in a golden period that lasted until he was forty. Through the 1980 PGA Tour season, Nicklaus solidified his reputation as the greatest player not only of his generation but of golf itself.

Between 1971 and 1980 he won nine major championships, an average of almost one a year. True, during these years Arnold Palmer and Gary Player declined as consistent rivals (though, of course, Player earned two green jackets, in 1974 and 1978), but Nicklaus was hardly lacking for strong competition in the majors. Beginning with his 1968 U.S. Open win, Lee Trevino was a force, and his heroics denied Nicklaus at least two majors. Tom Watson emerged in the mid-1970s, and he snatched the British Open away from Nicklaus at Turnberry in 1977. Johnny Miller won the U.S. Open in 1973, just ahead of Nicklaus, and had the talent to contend in every tournament he entered.

But Nicklaus was simply relentless. Even when he didn't win a major, he almost did. The U.S. Open during that period was a clear example. He was second in 1971, losing a playoff by two strokes to Trevino. He was fourth in 1973, three strokes behind Miller, who had closed with a record-setting

63. Jack finished only two strokes back in the 1975 Open. And he was four strokes off the pace in 1978.

The wins, not the close calls, made him the most intimidating player of that period. During the decade he won eighteen times on the PGA Tour, and at least as many non-Tour events around the world, and he was the most formidable force for British and then all European players to face in the Ryder Cup matches. And it was the rare major that didn't have the leader—if it wasn't Nicklaus himself—looking over his shoulder on Sunday to see how close the Golden Bear was.

Even in 1971, a year that Nicklaus might not have considered fully successful because he did not win a major, he played in twenty-three official worldwide tournaments, won eight, and had seventeen top-five finishes. He also went 5-1-0 in the Ryder Cup.

Still, he felt motivated to make 1972 different. He also unveiled a sleek new look with fashionably longer blond hair. He resembled a surfer more than a bear.

Midway through the year, the modern Grand Slam seemed not only within reach but inevitable. Nicklaus followed his Masters victory with a win at the U.S. Open, with Bruce Crampton three behind, Palmer four strokes back, and Homero Blancas and Trevino five shots out of first. That success tied Nicklaus with Walter Hagen for eleven professional majors won and Bobby Jones for thirteen overall. As at Augusta National, at Pebble Beach he had led after every round. His fellow competitors must have seen themselves as little more than future victims at the British Open and the PGA Championship, when the Hagen and Jones records would surely be erased.

It was not to be. At the British Open, in one of his most frustrating defeats, Nicklaus shot a fourth-round 66 but fell one shot short as Trevino won his second consecutive Claret Jug. And Gary Player showed that he still had plenty of game when he took the 1972 PGA Championship. Still, Nicklaus was again named PGA Player of the Year.

In 1973 he secured a Career Grand Slam for the second time when he captured the PGA Championship, a particularly satisfying win because it had looked like Nicklaus might end the year without a major championship in his bag, and instead he established a new record for career majors. His twelfth win as a professional gave him one more than Walter Hagen, and his two U.S. Amateur Championships gave him fourteen majors overall, eclipsing Bobby Jones's record of thirteen. He had seven tour victories overall and was crowned Player of the Year yet again, an honor that also recognized Nicklaus as the first golfer to exceed two million dollars in official earnings.

Jack's march on history slowed in 1974, when he secured only two PGA Tour wins and placed second to Miller on the money list. However, though only thirty-four, he was inducted into the World Golf Hall of Fame. (Unlike in some other sports—baseball, for example—in golf one does not have to wait until after retirement to be a hall of fame selection.) Nicklaus was all the more motivated to collect majors the next year.

The 1975 Masters was his third win in three consecutive starts. At the U.S. Open that year at the Medinah Country Club in Illinois, he was paired with Arnold Palmer, who at forty-five was having his last real hurrah at the event; Jack was closing in on first place on Sunday but fell two strokes short of a playoff that was won the next day by Lou Graham. Then at the British Open, he missed a playoff with Jack Newton and eventual winner Tom Watson by just one shot. Those close calls would appear even closer after he won the PGA Championship at the Firestone Country Club in Ohio. He tied Ben Hogan's record by being named PGA Player of the Year for the fourth time.

Although he didn't corral a major championship in 1976, it was a successful year for Nicklaus, ending with a record fifth Player of the Year trophy. A slight blemish was that he missed his first cut in a PGA tournament since 1970; his streak of 105 events was eight short of the record set by Byron Nelson.

But that same year a dream came true for Nicklaus. Eight years earlier, he had announced that he was going to build his own golf course in his hometown. In July 1972, workers broke ground outside Columbus, Ohio, for what would become Muirfield Village, a course inspired by Muirfield in Scotland. It was a massive effort to which Nicklaus had to devote precious time and money while raising a family with Barbara and, while he was at it, holding on to his crown as best golfer in the world.

"What finally carried the day was blind, pig-headed, cloth-eared, head-in-the-sand, Teutonic stubbornness, plus large amounts of thought, sweat and salesmanship along with many sleepless nights," he recalled in *Jack Nicklaus: My Story*. "The stubbornness was my contribution. The rest came from the friends and business associates I dragged into the nightmare."

The payoff came in May 1976 when the first Memorial Tournament was played at Muirfield Village. It remains one of the more popular events on the PGA Tour.

Nicklaus won the inaugural Memorial Tournament—which, oddly, prompted him to consider retiring from competitive golf. He had achieved victory at his own tournament in front of a hometown crowd, which made him wonder if he had accomplished as much as he could ask for. Perhaps this possibility nagged at him, because he came up short at the majors in 1977. But all was well again at St. Andrews in 1978 when Nicklaus played brilliant golf to win the British Open.

It was an especially emotional victory. As the broadcaster Jack Whitaker reported in a *New York Times* essay, "When he won, he received one of the most dramatic and moving ovations I have ever heard or seen. Thousands rose to their feet in the grandstands along the way. Ben Crenshaw, on the terrace of the clubhouse, joined the applause as it rose up over that old town, across the buildings of the University, which would later give Jack an honorary degree and the Freedom of the Town, an honor bestowed on only two other Americans, Benjamin Franklin and Bobby Jones."

The British Open victory meant that he had lapped himself by winning a Career Grand Slam for the third time.

But then came another slump, and as Nicklaus neared forty, more than a few fans and columnists thought that he was gradually riding into the sunset of a once-glowing career. In 1978 Nicklaus entered only fifteen PGA Tour events, and three fewer than that in 1979. His scoring average soared to 72.49, the highest of his career. He had no victories; in fact, his best showing was one third-place finish. His earnings plummeted to $59,434.

Well, he'd had a good run, the best ever. Most athletes don't excel in their forties, and that was true (then) of golfers too. Turning forty that January, perhaps Jack would look at the 1980 season as a fond farewell to the fans and his relieved rivals.

18

By the end of the day on Friday at the 1986 Masters, it was clear that Seve Ballesteros had followed through on his determination. He had kept the ball below the pin at sixteen of the eighteen greens. His best hole of the day was 15—his second shot with a 4-wood traveled 230 yards and landed on the green twenty-five feet below the hole, and he sank it for an eagle. And on the eighteenth hole he faced a slippery putt of eighteen feet, downhill. He drained it to card a four-under 68. His two-day total of 139 put him in the lead by a stroke.

In second was Bill Kratzert, who was successful in showing the crowd that his first-round 68 was not a fluke. His 72 gave him a 140 total after thirty-six holes. With Tommy Nakajima third at 141 with a workmanlike 71, Kratzert was the only American in the top three. It was remarkable that Nakajima was at Augusta National at all, after the spectacle of scoring a 13 on the thirteenth hole in his introduction to the Masters in 1978. A player with less fortitude would have fled down Magnolia Lane in a hurry, never to return.

As expected, the other high-profile foreign players not only made the cut but were sniffing the top of the leaderboard. Chief among them was Greg Norman, in the thick of the hunt with a 72 and a 142 total, three strokes

109

behind Ballesteros. It could have been worse. Norman double-bogeyed the tenth hole, needing four putts to put the ball in the cup. But displaying true grit, he didn't let the rest of the round slip away, carding birdies on 15 and 16. He did bogey the eighteenth, a gaffe that would play a crucial role later in the tournament.

Also at 142 after thirty-six holes were Bernhard Langer, journeyman Danny Edwards, Ben Crenshaw, and T. C. Chen. Langer had been especially impressive, with fifty-foot birdie putts on 10 and 16, the last one prompting the usually reserved West German to fall backward. With a round-ending birdie that gave him a 68, he showed his ball some well-deserved love by plucking it out of the cup and kissing it.

Four very good players were at 143—Mark McCumber, Corey Pavin, Bob Tway, and Gary Koch—but only Tway had ever won a major, and Koch's two-over 74 had been a disappointing step back. The curse of the Par 3 Contest was beginning to have an effect.

Tom Watson had begun the back nine with a birdie but overall had an up-and-down nine holes that included a double bogey at 12 for a 74 and a 144 total. For a veteran winner of majors, as Watson was, five strokes out of the lead with thirty-six more holes to play was close enough.

Idling at 144 with Watson were Tom Kite, Johnny Miller, and a resilient Donnie Hammond. Perhaps it wouldn't be that rough a weekend for U.S. golfers if at least a couple of these guys could make a move on Saturday— assuming Ballesteros didn't switch on the afterburners and leave everyone in the dust.

Jack Nicklaus continued to struggle with his putter on the back nine on Friday, making only three birdies when he'd had twelve putts under fifteen feet from the hole. "I was really down on myself for shooting 74 [yesterday] because I played pretty well, but I didn't make any putts; I didn't putt very well," Jack told reporters. "And then [today] I hit the ball pretty well, maybe a couple of little putts, not much, but shot 71, which wasn't any big deal."

He might not have been particularly impressed with his round, but it actually was a big deal, because the 145 thirty-six-hole total allowed him to make the cut with room to spare, and that left him in a position to possibly be a factor over the weekend. It was good news for the fans of the forty-six-year-old five-time former champion, many of whom had been observing him at Augusta National for twenty-seven years.

It was almost heroic that at his age and with a balky putter, Nicklaus managed even to be part of a few conversations on Friday night. After all, because of the many younger (and by now stronger) players and the power-ful foreign contingent, the odds of Jack beating them all seemed too high to overcome. That was the way many reporters would have it in the Saturday-morning editions of their newspapers. These articles and columns did not wind up on the refrigerator door, but the Golden Bear, sniffing the wind, knew what they were writing. In the third round, he would either prove them right or make them eat their words.

THE THIRD ROUND

Saturday, April 12

19

For forty members of the original field that teed off after Sarazen and Snead on Thursday, Saturday was not moving-up day but moving-out day—out of their hotel rooms and out of town for those poor fellows who hadn't made the cut.

It could be worse. Imagine how the players felt who hadn't made the cut at the Deposit Guaranty Golf Classic, a PGA Tour event held in Hattiesburg, Mississippi, the same week as the Masters and featuring those tour players who hadn't been invited to Augusta National. It might not be the most prestigious event, but it was an official one; it offered opportunity to younger players as well as older ones trying to hang on to their PGA Tour cards, and the payoff was real money. At the top of the leaderboard in 1986 were Rocco Mediate, Dan Halldorson, Tom Byrum, Paul Azinger, and Mike Miles. Among those who had missed the cut after thirty-six holes were David Peoples, Jim Dent, Blaine McCallister, Lance Ten Broeck (who would go on to have a successful career as a caddie), and Gary Cooper (no relation to the legendary actor).

Back at the Masters, some very big names were not going to play at Augusta National on Saturday. One was the 1982 Masters champion, Craig Stadler. Another was the 1976 winner, Raymond Floyd. The two-time U.S.

Open winner Hale Irwin also hadn't made the cut, nor had a previous PGA Championship winner, Hal Sutton. Also packing his bags was the highly regarded amateur Scott Verplank. Others who failed to qualify for a shot at a green jacket included past Masters champions Gay Brewer, George Archer, Charles Coody, Bob Goalby, Doug Ford, Tommy Aaron, and Billy Casper. Most of them would be found at the following weekend's Senior PGA Tour event.

There had been poignant moments on Friday when the two greatest past champions competing this year (other than Nicklaus) walked off 18 knowing they would not be around for the weekend. Gary Player looked like he might make the cut with a 150 total. But when his playing partner in his last Masters victory in 1978, Seve Ballesteros, birdied the eighteenth late on Friday, that set the cut line at 149. The great champion from South Africa had been in twenty-nine Masters Tournaments, and in 1986 he missed the cut for only the third time.

And at the age of fifty-six, Arnold Palmer was out as well. Maybe his 76 wasn't so bad, but following the 80 on Thursday, his 156 total missed the cut by seven strokes.

A silver lining to such well-known and in most cases veteran players not surviving after thirty-six holes was that it helped to refute the argument that the Masters was the easiest major because it was held at the same course every year. If Augusta were all that easy and familiar, then why couldn't past champions like Floyd and Stadler at least shoot 149? Every year variables like wind and course changes presented new challenges, and once again Augusta National had proven to be a tougher opponent than some players anticipated.

On Saturday, however, the weather would not be a formidable foe. It was warm and humid and overcast, but the wind that had bedeviled some golfers had expired. The combination of humid air and the watering done during the night would result in slower greens. Augusta National was more vulnerable to attack than usual.

Perhaps not every one of the forty-eight players who prepared to tee off for the third round thought they had a very good chance to win the Masters. Those who had not won a major championship before and were more than

A jubilant Jack Nicklaus after sinking the putt on the seventeenth hole that put him in the lead on Sunday.

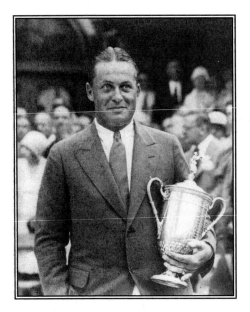

Robert Tyre Jones Jr. won the U.S. Open en route to the Grand Slam in 1930, and then he retired. He and Clifford Roberts founded the Augusta National Golf Club, where the tournament that would be known as the Masters was first held in 1934.
COURTESY OF THE U.S. GOLF ASSOCIATION

When Gene Sarazen won the 1935 tournament at Augusta National, which featured his dramatic double eagle in the final round, he became the first player to complete the modern Career Grand Slam: Masters, U.S. and British Opens, and the PGA Championship.
COURTESY OF THE U.S. GOLF ASSOCIATION

Sam Snead was the first player to receive a green jacket for a Masters victory, a tradition that began in 1949. Here the previous year's winner, Claude Harmon, helps the Slammer try it on.
COURTESY OF THE U.S. GOLF ASSOCIATION

A changing of the guard: Arnold Palmer congratulates Jack Nicklaus after the latter won the 1962 U.S. Open in a playoff, the first of Nicklaus's eighteen professional major championships. COURTESY OF THE U.S. GOLF ASSOCIATION

Early in his career Jack Nicklaus had already amassed an impressive collection of trophies, which he displays here with his father, Charlie Nicklaus.
COURTESY OF THE U.S. GOLF ASSOCIATION

Gary Player, who usually wore black, was the third member of the great triumvirate that ruled golf beginning in the late 1950s. He, Palmer, and Nicklaus won a total of thirteen Masters Championships.

Palmer's dramatic win in the 1964 Masters would be his fourth and final victory at Augusta National as well as his last major championship. COURTESY OF THE U.S. GOLF ASSOCIATION

Palmer, the 1964 Masters champion, helps Nicklaus into his second green jacket in 1965. Also present in the Butler Cabin for the traditional ceremony are (left to right) Downing Gray, the lowest-scoring amateur in the tournament; the 1961 champion, Gary Player; and tournament cofounders Clifford Roberts and Bobby Jones.

COURTESY OF THE U.S. GOLF ASSOCIATION

It was an especially satisfying victory for Jack and Barbara Nicklaus when he won the British Open in 1970 at St. Andrews, which had become Jack's favorite course outside the United States. COURTESY OF THE U.S. GOLF ASSOCIATION

After Nicklaus won the U.S. Open at Baltusrol in 1980, fans shouted, "Jack is back!" He also won the PGA Championship that year for what seemed like his last major championship. COURTESY OF THE U.S. GOLF ASSOCIATION

The charismatic and dynamic Seve Ballesteros had his third green jacket in his grasp down the stretch in the final round of the 1986 Masters. COURTESY OF THE *AUGUSTA CHRONICLE*

The thirteenth hole at Augusta National, the par-5 Azalea, where in April 1986 the Nicklaus charge over the last six holes began, astonishing screaming and shouting patrons. COURTESY OF THE U.S. GOLF ASSOCIATION

Greg Norman, on his way to becoming the number one golfer in the world, played a heroic back nine to tie Nicklaus for the lead. COURTESY OF THE *AUGUSTA CHRONICLE*

Texan Tom Kite had emerged as one of the best golfers in the world, and in the 1986 Masters he was one putt away from his first major championship.

COURTESY OF THE *AUGUSTA CHRONICLE*

Bernhard Langer, the 1985 winner, and a triumphant Jack Nicklaus in his sixth green jacket, during Sunday evening's closing ceremony.

COURTESY OF THE *AUGUSTA CHRONICLE*

Barbara and Jack Nicklaus have given back to golf in many ways, including raising millions of dollars for charities. In July 2010, they celebrated their fiftieth wedding anniversary.

COURTESY JIM MANDEVILLE/THE NICKLAUS COMPANIES

six shots out were more likely hoping for a good enough showing on Saturday and Sunday to finish as one of the top twenty-four scorers, the happy result being an automatic invitation to return to Augusta in 1987.

Those who hadn't won a major but were close enough to the top had to be thinking green jacket: Corey Pavin, Mark McCumber, T. C. Chen, Greg Norman, Tom Kite, and even Bill Kratzert, Danny Edwards, and Tommy Nakajima, who thus far had not had much success on the PGA Tour (though Nakajima had in Asian events). Brimming with confidence were Seve Ballesteros, Ben Crenshaw, Bernhard Langer, and even Tom Watson and Johnny Miller, although both were five strokes back. They knew from experience that the best shot at winning the Masters was to be in a good position already when the third round began and then truly take advantage of moving-up day.

Of the American players, Watson could be seen as having the advantage because of his previous wins in major championships, especially his two green jackets. He would see it that way too, looking back at the 1986 Masters twenty-four years later. "I was always nervous teeing it up at Augusta. I don't think any player loses that, especially if you're in contention on the weekend," recalls Watson. "But after winning the first one, you get the proverbial monkey off your back. It becomes, 'I've won it; let's go out and win it again. I know how to win here.' You get into that confidence that you know how to win. That means a lot to starting a round in the right frame of mind."

The Golden Bear was lurking close behind the pack. But perhaps not close enough to really make an impression. "A general feeling was that Jack had done well enough to make the cut at his age, and that was the peak of the tournament for him," recalls sports broadcaster Verne Lundquist, who was stationed at the seventeenth hole during the CBS coverage that weekend. "As far as actually being in a position to win the tournament, he wasn't on anyone's radar screen."

"Yes, that was the general thought," agrees Pat Summerall, who covered the eighteenth hole for the CBS telecast, "that Jack was not a serious contender. He made the cut, but that's as far as it's going. He had his son caddying for him, and maybe for sentimental reasons you thought there could be a chance. But that was about the extent of it."

Ron Green's assessment in the *Charlotte Observer* smacked of a "thanks for the memories" send-off: "The fact is, Palmer, who shockingly flubbed two shots on Thursday the way we might en route to missing the 36-hole cut, and Player, who shot 77-73 and was also dismissed, are simply making curtain calls. Nicklaus is approaching that status, having won no title of any kind in two years. He's not out of it this week, not at all, but he is no longer menacing, just close enough to give us hope that in the next two days he will suddenly find what he has, that he will be young one more time."

As for Jack himself, his philosophy was not to fret over how many strokes he was out of first place when the third and then fourth rounds began but to focus on how many players were in front of him. He had to be somewhat encouraged when he eyed the leaderboard before the beginning of play on Saturday morning. Sixteen players were ahead of Jack, but among them were Kratzert, Nakajima, and Donnie Hammond—good players but not ones whom he had to fear. He knew that on Saturday at Augusta National it was as much about players slipping down as it was about others moving up, and that veteran champions like him would do well to stay close and not worry about a must-have low score.

When the gates opened early Saturday morning, the patrons who flooded in expected a good contest with plenty of dramatics to come. Probably, though, not even the eternal optimists among them anticipated witnessing the most memorable Masters ever.

20

Right before the 1986 Masters began, Raymond Floyd had stated to Will Grimsley of the *New York Times*, "It's the tournament every golfer most wants to win."

While few would argue, the press appeared to think that the foreign players wanted it more and that such a winner was inevitable at Augusta National. "Our lads are squirming a bit now," Furman Bisher of the *Atlanta Journal-Constitution* wrote after the third round. "Professional American golfers are becoming spoiled, soft from a tour endowment that leaves them awfully comfortable with their lot. There are 58 millionaires on the tour. Fifteen have won over two million."

The columnist pointed to all the foreign players at and near the top of the leaderboard, then continued: "Doing his best to hold his country's own among them is one solitary American, like the boy at the dike, Donnie Hammond of Daytona Beach, Fla., playing his first Masters five under par after first playing the role of security guard here a few years ago. Red is the color for the names of foreign players on the leaderboard here, and this one looks as if it has broken out with the measles."

Foreign or domestic, it was every man for himself during the early holes of the third round. Perhaps the likable Hammond had read or heard about

Bisher's "boy at the dike" comparison, because he initially appeared unfazed by the foreign competition. After hitting the stick with his approach shot on the second hole, he appeared to gain confidence. As his round continued, he gained some new fans too.

Hammond may not have been a household name, but of late he had been experiencing some success on the PGA Tour. The Jacksonville University graduate had turned professional seven years earlier, at twenty-two, and he had tied for sixteenth in the 1984 PGA Championship. Most impressive thus far was that just three months earlier, in January, he had shot five rounds in the 60s in the Bob Hope Chrysler Classic. He had finished dead even with John Cook at twenty-five under, then won the playoff for his first PGA Tour triumph. This Masters was Hammond's inaugural one and the only major he had played in other than the PGA Championship.

It was not, however, his first time at Augusta National: in 1975, as Bisher mentioned, he had worked there during the Masters as a gallery guard. "Every time I look up and see one of those guards, I give him a nod because I've been there," Hammond said in an interview with Brent Musburger and Tom Weiskopf, who were on the job for CBS.

Many thought that Seve Ballesteros was poised to pummel the golf course. Scoring conditions were favorable, he was in his prime, and three years after his second victory at Augusta National, it was just time for him to grab hold of another championship. He and Bill Kratzert made up the last group. When they arrived at the first tee, Ballesteros looked dashing and ready to go in a dark blue sweater over a crisp white shirt, wine-red pants, and white shoes, while Kratzert's bright red shirt would turn out to be a reflection of the red numbers he would post that afternoon.

But Ballesteros didn't burst out of the gate. Indeed, this would turn out to be a longer day than having to play gin rummy with Deane Beman. He parred the first and second holes. The short par-4 third hole was more to his liking. He pitched to four feet from the pin and sank the putt for birdie. He was back to par for the next three holes, though, and thus couldn't open up any space between himself and the rest of the field. It would not be 1980 again, when he was so far in front that on Sunday the rest of the players could barely see him and he became a bit bored. In fact, Ballesteros would find out that finishing his first six holes at one under on the day was close to being the peak of his round.

Meanwhile, the groups ahead of him were cutting and slashing, thinking that they had better do well from the beginning or Seve would be saying "adios" as he separated himself from the pack.

Greg Norman began the round playing steady but not particularly inspired golf. The expression on his long, handsome face indicated that he wasn't pleased with par golf during the first third of his round on a day when scoring conditions were very good. Bernhard Langer birdied the par-5 second hole, and that gave him confidence early in his round. Ben Crenshaw birdied 2 and 5 to go to four under par, behind only Ballesteros and Nick Price.

Tom Kite and Tom Watson, both thirty-six, were comfortable being partnered. While the latter had enjoyed a more successful career by winning the eight majors, Kite had done well too, as one of the PGA Tour's top money earners for years. Both were low-key on the course, and their demeanor didn't change early in the round when a couple of birdies implied they could have a very satisfying day. Mark McCumber caused the most excitement early in his round when he eagled 2 and birdied 4.

Nicklaus's plan to get an aggressive start looked like it was being implemented when he birdied the second hole. He parred 3 and 4. One under par for four holes was fine if he could do that three more times and be four under on the day as he stood on the seventeenth tee. But he bogeyed the fifth hole and parred the sixth, so one-third of the way through the round he had not advanced from where he was at the end of Friday.

There was nothing Jackie could say. He also knew that if his father ran in place on Saturday, Sunday's round would be nothing more than a formality and there would be more grating references to the Olden Bear.

21

Nothing announced louder that players from around the world, especially those from Europe, were ready to challenge the American domination of golf when the decade began than the way that Seve Ballesteros had dismantled Augusta National six years earlier.

By 1980, Ballesteros had already earned a major championship, the 1979 British Open, and was obviously hungry for one of those held in the United States. Apparently, being only twenty-three didn't make him believe that he should show more respect for his golfing elders. As Dan Jenkins put it in his coverage: "Seve Ballesteros seemed to be playing in a different tournament from everyone else in the 1980 Masters, including most of the recognizable American stars, unless of course you happen to be a close follower of those golfing legends Jeff Mitchell, Rex Caldwell, Ed Fiori, and Gibby Gilbert."

Nicklaus? Trevino? Watson? Miller? Any of the other top-shelf U.S. players? Nowhere to be found at the end of play on Sunday, except for Fuzzy Zoeller, whose only reason for still being at Augusta National Sunday evening was to help Ballesteros into his green jacket.

It had to help that even at such a tender age Ballesteros was not a rookie in the Masters. In 1977, when he was twenty, he had received his first invitation to Augusta National. The young Spaniard had just finished second to

Johnny Miller in the British Open at Royal Birkdale. Miller was impressed, and he made the generous gesture of writing to the Tournament Committee suggesting that Ballesteros receive an invitation. Symbolically, invitations came to him and other leaders of a new generation of foreign players the same year that Clifford Roberts died.

"Augusta was love at first sight," wrote Ballesteros in *Seve: The Official Autobiography*. "I was smitten. I felt at ease right from the start and even in my first interviews I was telling reporters that the course was just right for my style of play. I also said I was sure I would win the Masters some day, which was a reflection of how much I liked the course and how confident I was it would bring out the best in my game."

In his very first round in the 1977 Masters, he was paired with Jack Nicklaus. Ballesteros made the cut but did not finish as one of the top twenty-four players in the tournament. Still, the club was intrigued enough to invite him back, and in the 1978 Masters he partnered with Gary Player—exactly twice his age—during the South African's stunning back-nine 30 on Sunday to win the championship. Ballesteros tied for twelfth in the 1979 tournament, earning another invitation. Many observers sensed that the time had come for him to win in Augusta, especially after he won that year's British Open.

So did Ballesteros: "It may seem arrogant, but when I reached Augusta that year [1980] I was already expecting to win the Masters."

He didn't disappoint. Right from the beginning, it was as though Ballesteros had been launched out of a cannon; on Thursday, he carded a 66. Remarkably, this earned him only a tie for first, with Mitchell and the Australian David Graham. On Friday, Mitchell and Graham fell by the wayside along with most others when Ballesteros shot a 69 and took a four-stroke lead. At the end of the third round he was seven shots ahead thanks to a 68 and no one giving much of a chase.

If golf had a mercy rule, it would have been imposed at some point during the final round—most likely after the front nine, when Ballesteros held a ten-shot lead. Perhaps the leader became put off by the lack of challengers, because he began to record bogeys. Echoing Roberto De Vicenzo a bit, though the context was much different, Ballesteros could be heard muttering, "You stupid! What are you doing?"

But while he was questioning his golf IQ, no rival took advantage of the lackadaisical play. Ballesteros still won by four strokes and was thirteen under par for the tournament. He took from Nicklaus the distinction of being the youngest Masters winner ever, at three months younger than the Golden Bear was in April 1963. Perhaps more remarkable, this Masters was already the twenty-fifth tournament Ballesteros had won worldwide, and he had won the British Order of Merit—equivalent to the top money earner of the PGA Tour—three consecutive years.

Though the field had surrendered pretty early on, it could have been worse. Ask Tom Weiskopf. He became notable for the wrong reason after recording a total of twenty strokes on the twelfth hole: thirteen on Thursday and seven on Friday. As Jenkins concluded, "Rae's Creek overflowed with Weiskopf's Titleists." No wonder he made the shift to broadcasting.

After the 1980 tournament, Nicklaus concluded that of all the players around, Ballesteros had the best chance of winning as many majors as he had—quite a weight to place on anyone's shoulders. For most of the decade, Seve could carry it.

The leaderboard of the 1981 Masters could be viewed as a reaction to the Spanish/European victory of the year before. Of the top ten finishers, only two were foreigners and neither one was European—Greg Norman and David Graham were from Australia.

This Masters was the first one contested on bent grass greens, and thus whoever could putt best on the new surfaces had an advantage. Or maybe you just had to be a darn good player. Johnny Miller shot a 69 in the opening round, as did Greg Norman and Curtis Strange. The second round belonged to Jack Nicklaus, who blistered the course with a 65. Also getting good results on Friday were Bruce Lietzke with a 67, past champion Gay Brewer with a 68, and another former champion, Tom Watson, also with a 68, which gave him the lead. Saturday was a tough one for going low, with only John Mahaffey and Bob Gilder breaking 70 among the top twenty. Nicklaus trudged off the eighteenth green having shot ten strokes higher than his second round.

On Sunday, it boiled down to whether Watson could hold on to the lead he had stubbornly clung to in the third round. He was being assailed on all sides. Raymond Floyd scored a 69 to enter the clubhouse with a 286 total, tied with Mahaffey and Ben Crenshaw. Graham's 71 and 285 were not enough. Tom Kite carded a 68 to tie with Jerry Pate at 284. Norman could do no better than par and finished at 283. Neither could Nicklaus, who ended the tournament one stroke better, at 282.

For a time, Johnny Miller looked like the player who had shot a sizzling 63 in the final round to win the U.S. Open eight years earlier, and his 68 on Sunday at Augusta National had him in the clubhouse tied for the lead with Nicklaus. But Watson just kept grinding and averting land mines. His 71 was not spectacular by any means, but it was enough for 280 and a two-stroke victory. It was the last time Nicklaus would be a runner-up in the Masters.

A nice footnote to the tournament was that the lowest score posted by a foreign player after Norman and Graham was by Gary Player, at 288, allowing him another top-ten finish, at the age of forty-five.

To many observers at the 1982 Masters, Craig Stadler looked too out of shape to be a caddie let alone a successful professional golfer, but there was no better illustration of the saying "Looks can be deceiving." He gutted out a victory by winning in a playoff over Dan Pohl, who had played excellent golf over the final two rounds after barely making the cut on Friday.

Known for his temper as much as his girth—and, of course, for his nickname, Walrus—Stadler, who grew up in La Jolla, California, was seventeen when he won the 1971 World Junior Championship. He was a standout at the University of Southern California and was twenty when he won the U.S. Amateur Championship. That triumph earned him an invitation to his first Masters in 1974. His temper more than his weight hurt him during the rest of the decade, although he reported after he lost thirty pounds, "I didn't feel comfortable putting at 195, maybe because I didn't have the gut in my way."

Stadler earned a satisfying $206,291 in 1980 and upped that to $218,829 the next year. It looked like he had gotten in the right groove temperamentally as well—good thing, because he was sorely tested at Augusta National in 1982. He managed to stay near the top of the leaderboard during the first thirty-six holes, then took control on that Saturday with three closing birdies that resulted in a 67 and a three-stroke lead.

But Sunday was a different story. Stadler struggled—as he had in the 1979 Masters when he lost the lead in the final round—with four bogeys on the back nine that included the final hole. He kept his temper after grinding out a 73, which could not have happened at a better time because Pohl had caught him to force the playoff. He parred the tenth hole, the first one of the playoff, and when Pohl didn't, Stadler squeezed into a size 46 regular green jacket presented to him by Watson.

At the 1983 Masters, a controversy from the previous year's event resulted in a big change at Augusta National: players were allowed to use their own caddies for the first time.

Many players prefer the relationship with their regular caddies and thus forgo having strangers on their bags during major championships. While it was not unusual for players to use local caddies in the British Open because of their intimate knowledge of courses like St. Andrews and Royal Birkdale, they were not required to. And while early on, the U.S. Open and PGA Championship had banned "outside" caddies, both events had dropped that rule many years before. So another way the Masters had been unique was that only Augusta National caddies could be used in the tournament. That meant for almost half a century Ironman, Cemetery, Eight Ball, Bodiddley, Shoo Poon, Long Distance, Wheezy, Marble Eye, and the other colorfully nicknamed caddies were the only men allowed to be on the bags of Masters participants.

It is unlikely that this Masters rule would have changed during the lifetime of Clifford Roberts, but by 1983 he had been dead for over five years. In the 1982 Masters, rain on Friday had forced the second round to be completed on Saturday. Some players complained that their equipment had not been adequately dried off from the night before, and a few of the caddies were late reporting for work for the early resumption of action on Saturday. Combined with more players in recent years asking to use their own caddies, the 1982 controversy was the tipping point, and the Tournament Committee got rid of the "home" caddie rule. According to Hord Hardin, the chairman, "It was a difficult decision to make, but it was the only fair thing to do."

In the 1983 edition of the Masters, some players continued to use Augusta National caddies. Jack Nicklaus, for example, was using Willie

Peterson again, but then Peterson was sidelined when Nicklaus withdrew from the tournament on Friday because of back spasms. Other players took immediate advantage of their freedom of choice. George Archer made history by hiring his nineteen-year-old daughter, Elizabeth, the first woman to caddie in the Masters.

Even though Tom Watson had earned his two green jackets with Leon McClattie on the bag, he was typical of the players who brought their regular tour caddies with them. "After playing in the Masters for 10 years, I know the yardage and I know the club," he told Dave Anderson of the *New York Times*. "Bruce [Edwards, his longtime caddie] doesn't know the course that well yet, but he knows me."

There was still plenty of work for the club's caddies the rest of the year that Augusta National was open, but some of them viewed the Tournament Committee's decision as a step back. They certainly took a hit financially.

It was a common practice that a caddie receive 10 percent of his player's earnings. (In the case of a player's regular tour caddie, this was in addition to whatever weekly salary agreement had been negotiated.) So, for example, since the first-place check in the previous Masters had been sixty-four thousand dollars, Craig Stadler's caddie, an employee of the club, probably received sixty-four hundred, which added substantially to what he made that year in salary and tips. That was true for every caddie whose player finished in the top twenty-four, because not only were those players the higher earners in the tournament but they also earned an invitation back to the Masters the following year, when presumably they would want to repeat or better their good performance by using the same caddie.

The caddie change also had the unintentional effect of reducing the number of black faces on the course during Masters week. Augusta National had employed only African Americans as caddies, so for the first time in forty-seven tournaments, some of the caddies were white. Some players had African Americans as their regular caddies, but many did not. Calvin Peete—whose PGA Tour career would include twelve victories, and a tie for eleventh in 1986 would be his best Masters finish—was one of the very few African American golfers to play in the championship. Even though information about membership was never discussed outside the committee, most knew that the Augusta National Golf Club had yet to invite its first black member. (To this day, the number of Augusta National members and the cost of joining remain the equivalent of state secrets.)

Race had already been a significant issue at the club. It would be one throughout the sport in the United States during the 1980s, culminating in the threat of boycotts at the PGA Championship at Crooked Stick in Indiana in 1991 (where John Daly's improbable win drowned out the racial headlines). The Masters Tournament Committee had most prominently faced the issue in 1973 when it did not invite Lee Elder, a black golfer, to play. Roberts had to respond to a stern letter from the U.S. Congress about what appeared to be a deliberate omission.

Elder had tied with Lee Trevino after seventy-two holes in the 1972 Greater Hartford Open, then lost the playoff. Roberts pointed out that if Elder had won the playoff, by the Masters eligibility rules he would have received an invitation no matter what color he was. A week after the 1974 Masters, Elder won a playoff, this one in the Monsanto Open over Peter Oosterhuis. Hence, he was invited to play in the 1975 Masters.

According to David Owen's book *The Making of the Masters*, "Officially, Roberts had said that Elder would be accorded no special treatment for the Masters. Unofficially, he and the club made numerous efforts behind the scenes to make Elder's experience easier—for example, by issuing him twice the number of tournament guest tickets that were normally allocated to competitors." Owen also reported, "Elder was assigned a veteran caddie named Henry Brown, who himself was an accomplished player and had once shot 68 on the course."

Elder remembered, "I was so nervous, I was shaking. I arrived in a limo and Cliff Roberts met me at the front gate. It was like a three-ring circus. It took an hour to get from the locker room to the putting green, I was asked so many questions."

It was drizzling on April 10, 1975, when Elder teed off for the first time in a Masters. He was certainly attired for a nicer day—white visor, light green sweater, and dark green pants. When the forty-year-old Dallas native hit his tee shot—which found the middle of the fairway—the Augusta National racial barrier was broken. Elder shot a 152 and missed the cut that year, as

Nicklaus won his fifth green jacket, but he kept earning more invitations. He made three cuts in the six Masters he played; in his best outing he tied for seventeenth in 1979, when he was forty-four.

Gene Littler played with Elder during the historic first round in 1975. "We just went out and played golf," he told the *Dallas Morning News*. "Nothing happened. Nothing was said. Obviously, it was a big deal for him, and we appreciated that. But I think both of us just tried to make it another round at Augusta."

From that point on, it was clear that players of any color, religion, or nationality would be invited to be part of the Masters as long as they had played their way into eligibility. It should be noted, however, that it was not until 1990 that the Augusta National Golf Club admitted its first black member. And while there have been several female caddies in Masters Tournaments, to this day the club does not admit women as members. This issue was put in the spotlight in 2003 when Martha Burk, head of the National Council of Women's Organizations, criticized Augusta National for the absence of female members. Club officials rejected the criticism, and Burk's call for prominent players to support her position fell on deaf ears.

In addition to the new caddie rule, another noteworthy change was in the air at the 1983 Masters: it was the last one to feature Sam Snead as a competitor. By virtue of his three victories, he could have continued to play as long as he could walk, with no need to requalify or seek exemptions as in other majors. He had certainly aged well—his last PGA Tour victory was in 1965, years after other triumvirate members Byron Nelson and Ben Hogan had collected their last titles. He had even won the Par 3 Contest at Augusta National twice, the second time at sixty-one.

In January 1956, Snead had written in a letter to Roberts thanking him for all the invitations he had received (and certainly earned) over the years, "I hope I'll never be too old to want to take part in this event, and I don't think I will ever age that much." But by 1983, the reality of being seventy-one the month after the Masters had sunk in. He had last made a cut at Augusta National in 1974, when he was sixty-one.

Snead played thirty-six holes in his forty-fourth and final Masters. "I'm no longer a competitor out here," he admitted. "I haven't made the cut in so long. It's that time." Thus, the last member of the triumvirate that had begun playing the Masters in the 1930s went into retirement.

The Slammer stayed to watch the weekend action unfold, as an honored guest among the patrons and Augusta National Golf Club members. While it wasn't quite a repeat of 1980 because the lead when Sunday began wasn't as large, the outcome was the same: Seve Ballesteros being helped into a green jacket, this time by Stadler.

Stadler, Raymond Floyd, and Tom Watson had fought the Spaniard toe-to-toe up to Sunday, then faded in the final round. The Texas two, Ben Crenshaw and Tom Kite, took over and challenged Ballesteros by recording a 68 and 69 and finishing tied at four under par. Ballesteros had begun the round at five under. His rivals had to hope he would stumble.

Instead, he came out of the gate like a stallion. For the first four holes he had birdie, eagle, par, and birdie, taking him to nine under for the tournament. Kite observed, "That's like he was driving a Ferrari and the rest of us were driving Chevrolets. He blasted us." (Presumably, he was not offered a Chevy endorsement deal after this assessment.)

Poor Watson couldn't catch a break. On the par-4 fourteenth, his approach shot went bouncing haphazardly behind the green. A woman who was a newcomer to the tournament picked it up off the grass. Her husband was aghast. To cover her crime, she dropped the ball into her purse. Watson was charged with losing the ball and double-bogeyed the hole. His 73 on the round left him tied for fourth. Even without the interference he still might not have caught Ballesteros, but it was an expensive double bogey. Watson remained mystified about how the ball could have disappeared until he was sixty and playing in the 2010 Masters and the woman's by-then ex-husband approached him to explain the disappearance.

Ballesteros scored one bogey and the rest par for the remainder of the round, and his 69 gave him another four-stroke victory. He had turned twenty-six two days earlier, and as a present he was handed a ninety-thousand-dollar check, the highest first-place money in Masters history. A lot had changed for the Augusta National Golf Club financially in almost a half century.

"It's a great pity that a man like Seve Ballesteros is not an American," Gary Player commented. "He would be just marvelous for the tour because

I think he's a second Arnold Palmer. He got out of bed one day like Arnold Palmer and they were both born with that charisma."

The next year, Ben Crenshaw was "the most popular golfer since Arnold Palmer," according to Dan Jenkins. If indeed that was true, there would be no better place for him to win his first major than at the Augusta National Golf Club.

Crenshaw had been struggling through some tough times. Sometimes referred to as "the cute Jack Nicklaus," he had been one of the best collegiate golfers in the United States after shining at Austin High School along with varsity teammate Tom Kite. Crenshaw was expected to be one of the most successful players on the PGA Tour. Though he won some events and showed flashes of brilliance, that didn't happen. He finished five majors in second place, including being runner-up to Ballesteros in the 1983 Masters. He'd also been through a divorce and other woes. When the 1984 Masters began, many patrons and members of the press still had hopes for him, but they also sensed that he might end up in the category of best golfer never to win a major.

Crenshaw felt that his game, like his life, was turning around. He had just tied for third at Greensboro with a closing-round 67, and he felt more confident about competing at Augusta National than he had in the previous few years. In his memoir, *A Feel for the Game: To Brookline and Back*, he reflected, "Just where those four days came from, I'm not sure. I was tired of losing majors, that's certain. Nearly a dozen chances to win majors—and no titles—were beginning to put worries in my head, and Augusta was no place for that. But I was beginning to feel my way around this course really well and, for once, I came in relaxed and with one thing in mind—winning."

Which is what Crenshaw did, at last. Jenkins reported, "As the 32-year-old Texan walked up the last fairway on Sunday, you could have watered all the botanical wonders on the course with the tears of joy that were creeping down the cheeks of the thousands whose hopes he had crushed so often. In a way, this one was for them."

For sixty-three holes, Crenshaw had dueled a handful of rivals, especially Tom Kite, Tom Watson, and Larry Nelson. But on the tenth hole, he sank a sixty-footer for birdie. Then he birdied the twelfth while Kite triple-bogeyed and Nelson double-bogeyed, sending their hopes to the showers. Watson birdied 18 to put some pressure on the leader, but apparently not enough. Crenshaw's final-round 68 and his eleven-under 277 total were both two strokes better than Watson's scores.

"I've never masked my feelings about the game of golf," Crenshaw told reporters. "I genuinely love it. This is really a sweet, sweet victory, and I think it means more to me now than if I had won it ten years ago or so." Making it even sweeter was the first-place check, which had grown to $108,000.

Once again, Lee Trevino did not come close to winning the Masters in 1984. But he finally won an argument there. It rained during Saturday's round, and when he, George Archer, and David Graham reached the sixteenth green they found that it was covered with water. Trevino complained to a Masters official, who told the trio that they had to putt anyway.

Archer three-putted. Trevino was next, and he refused. He said to the official, "If you think I'm going to putt, you better call the clubhouse and get your lunch. We're going to be out here a while."

The official radioed tournament headquarters, told officials there about what Trevino later referred to as the "Mexican standoff," and turned back to Trevino to say that no matter what, he had to putt his ball. "Then you better call somebody else," Trevino said.

The official did: Clyde Mangum, the deputy commissioner of the PGA Tour. He agreed that Trevino was playing by the rules: if a player is on the putting surface and cannot move his ball to a dry surface to putt, the green has to be toweled or squeegeed, with play suspended until it is. And that was what happened.

"After they did the right thing, I wanted to show the television audience how deep the water was on the course," Trevino later reported. "So when I went to 17 I skipped along and dragged my club behind me. Water churned in my wake as if an outboard motorboat had just come through."

The 1984 Masters was also when Bernhard Langer made the cut for the first time. He had not won yet in the United States, though he had carved out a good career while only in his midtwenties with victories in Spain, France, and even Japan as well as his native Germany. His first invitation to Augusta National came in 1982. "Even though I had played golf around the world I had never encountered such fast and tricky greens," he recalled in the imaginatively titled *Bernhard Langer: My Autobiography*. He missed the cut that year by one stroke. Although he made it two years later, the best he could do was a tie for thirty-first.

Not surprisingly, for most of the 1985 Masters, Langer flew under the radar. He opened with a 72, leaving him four strokes behind the leader, Gary Hallberg. His 74 on Friday left him six strokes out of first place, which was amply occupied by Craig Stadler, looking for his second green jacket in four years, Tom Watson, and the knickered Payne Stewart.

But the far more remarkable story belonged to Curtis Strange. The Virginian had shot an 80 on the first eighteen holes, and that Thursday night he had to already be thinking about what to pack and where he was going to be for the weekend.

But Strange was a tough guy—he would win back-to-back U.S. Opens in 1988 and 1989, the only player other than Johnny McDermott and Bobby Jones to do so—and he bounced back with a terrific 65 on Friday and then 68 in the third round, which put him just one stroke behind Saturday's leader, Raymond Floyd, who had won his Masters nine years earlier. (Patrons were reminded of Dan Pohl, who barely made the cut with a 150 total in the 1982 Masters, then ended up in the playoff Sunday afternoon with Stadler.) When the back nine began on Sunday, Strange, who had blistered the course, had a four-stroke lead and rivals like Langer were in the rearview mirror.

They approached fast, though, thanks to Strange sending his second shots into the water on the thirteenth and fifteenth holes, both par-5s. Langer, partnered with Ballesteros, had put himself in the best position to take advantage of any faltering by the leader by birdieing 12, 13, and 15 and playing 10 through 17 at five under par. He bogeyed 18, though, and closed with a 68, but Strange never recovered. Langer won, becoming the third foreign player, after Gary Player and Ballesteros, to earn a Masters championship. "It was perhaps not the best day to wear red trousers and a red shirt," remembered Langer. "When the previous year's champion, Ben Crenshaw, put the green jacket on me, someone said that I looked like a Christmas tree!"

It wasn't happy holidays for Strange, who said afterward, "I'll go home and beat my head against the wall because deep down it hurts."

It was a different kind of hurt for the defending champion. Crenshaw had a new fiancée to keep his spirits up, but that was about it. His play in the 1985 Masters had been pretty dismal. It was as though the previous year's victory had been his last hurrah and he was finished at only thirty-three. He had lost as much as fifteen pounds since April 1984, and his ball striking was a mess. But he was a lucky man after all. After seeing a psychiatrist didn't turn things around, Crenshaw underwent a barrage of tests that revealed an overactive thyroid. Later, his ailment was narrowed down to Graves' disease, and he has been on medication for it ever since.

Going into the 1986 Masters, the favorites had to be the last three winners: Langer, a revived Crenshaw, and Ballesteros. The next generation had taken firm control of the tournament.

22

Nineteen seventy-nine was the first year without a win for Jack Nicklaus since he became a professional golfer. Startling evidence of his fall from the heights was his seventy-first-place finish on the PGA Tour money list after never having placed lower than fourth. He turned forty in January 1980, and after such a dreadful year it looked to many observers like the Golden Bear's eighteen-year professional career was winding down.

"Glibly as I'd talked about quitting golf over the years, as 1979 drew to a close I had to face the fact that it had truly become one of just two options," he reflected in *Jack Nicklaus: My Story*. "The other was to remake my swing."

Nicklaus chose to give competitive golf one more try. He felt in excellent physical condition, the idea of a 1980 comeback presented a challenge, and his mentor Jack Grout was available. He went to work in Florida with the man who still called him "Jackie boy" and would later write about those grueling weeks, "All in all, it was the hardest I had worked at golf since my teen years. But the big question remained: would it pay off?"

It didn't seem to. He lost in a playoff to Raymond Floyd at the Doral Open, which was actually encouraging, but his results in the next few tournaments were pretty dismal. They included a tie for thirty-third in the Masters that had the patrons there ready to send him sympathy cards. He missed the cut at the Atlanta Classic, but when he shot a 67 in the second round after a putting tip from Grout, it boosted his confidence going into the U.S. Open at one of his favorite courses, Baltusrol in New Jersey.

There, Nicklaus burst on the scene. Tom Weiskopf had gone out earlier and shot a 63, and Jack matched it. He had never shot such a low score in the first round of a major. The next day he carded a 71 for a thirty-six-hole total of 134. But Jack wasn't running away from the pack. Isao Aoki, from Japan, had put together back-to-back 68s.

Aoki proved to be a stubborn opponent. On Saturday, he shot another 68. That tied him with Nicklaus, who had totaled a 70. Nicklaus and Aoki were partnered all four days of the Open, and as the latter's English was minimal, the conversation consisted of "Nice putt" and the response "Thanks, Jack."

It came down to the final round on Sunday—Father's Day, when Nicklaus had won his three previous Opens. Aoki faltered, recording a 70, though he hung tough by birdieing the last two holes. Jack answered with birdies on 17 and 18 too, and his 68 earned him his fourth U.S. Open championship. The spectators had worked themselves into a frenzy already, and when his last putt dropped, Nicklaus had to restrain them with a raised-hands gesture so that Aoki could finish.

"But bedlam broke out again the second his ball vanished," Nicklaus reported in his autobiography, "to the point where it became quite scary as well as thrilling, particularly after I was accidentally kicked hard in the shin and could do no better than limp along as police and officials fought to clear out a passage to the scorers' tent."

The pain was worth it: he set a new low-scoring record of 272 in the U.S. Open. And along with that, Nicklaus became the only golfer to win the Open in three different decades.

Tom Watson lamented after the tournament, "I just shot 276, the fourth-lowest score in the history of the U.S. Open, and lost by four shots." It was worse for Aoki: no one since the Open was first held eighty-five years earlier had shot less than 275; the man from Japan had, by a stroke, yet still lost by two.

Why not a British Open while he was on the comeback trail? And it was at Muirfield, where Jack had won before. But standing in his way was a white-hot Tom Watson, and Nicklaus finished fourth, nine strokes back. It was back to the States and the next major challenge: the PGA Championship, being held at the Oak Hill Country Club in Rochester, New York.

It was no contest, and spectators and even a few members of the press were chanting, "Jack is back!" (During the Open at Baltusrol, an entrepreneur had made and sold hundreds of yellow T-shirts that proclaimed, "The Bear Is Back.") The runner-up, Andy Bean, was a distant seven shots back. Nicklaus was the only player to break par for the tournament—and, in an even more stark illustration of how strong his play was, he averaged 68.50 strokes, compared to 74.60 for the other players. Dan Jenkins wrote that Nicklaus had turned the tournament "into a hunting expedition in which you were supposed to find the rest of the field."

It was his fifth PGA Championship. This tied him with Walter Hagen, surely a big achievement, though one might still give Sir Walter the edge here because his victories were in match play and he won four consecutive championships.

Nicklaus became only the third player in history to win the U.S. Open and PGA Championship in the same year—Gene Sarazen had done it in 1922 and Ben Hogan in 1948. For Sarazen and Hogan, though, they had been breakthrough years that led to great careers; with Nicklaus, on the other hand, many thought the two victories were a fitting cap to his career. His total number of major championships stood at seventeen (counting the two U.S. Amateurs). If he was nearing the end of the trail, Jack was going out in a blaze of glory.

The next five years were not without their highlights. He was 4-0-0 in the 1981 Ryder Cup, his last year as a player in that event. He placed in the top ten in seven majors. But he won just two PGA Tour events, though one was particularly satisfying—becoming the first repeat champion in his own Memorial tourney in 1984. (In the Skins Game that year he earned his single biggest paycheck, $240,000.) And there were no more crowns in majors. He did finish second in three of them—the 1981 Masters, where he lost again to Tom Watson; the 1982 U.S. Open, where "Tom Terrific" outlasted him at Pebble Beach, helped by one of the most sensational chip shots in Open history, for birdie on 17 (afterward, Jack shook Watson's hand and said, affectionately, "You little son of a bitch, you did it to me again."); and the 1983 PGA Championship at Riviera in Los Angeles to Hal Sutton—but he was slipping backward. Even columnist Jim Murray, who was a friend, wrote a career obituary for him on the last day of the PGA event.

And every January, when he turned a year older, the likelihood became smaller that Jack would once again wear a green jacket, or hold a Claret Jug or Wanamaker Trophy, or become the first man to win five U.S. Opens.

Jack's experiences at Augusta National had to be especially frustrating. He had enjoyed winning three championships there in four years in the 1960s, and two more championships in the first half of the next decade. But after 1975, he'd had nothing but a few close calls.

It didn't get better in the 1980s. The outcome of the 1981 tournament was an indication that Nicklaus would find winning a Masters and probably any of the other major championships increasingly elusive. He had begun Sunday's round in first by four strokes, helped largely by that second-round 65. With Tom Watson second, it looked like long-overdue payback time for the major Watson whisked out from under him at Turnberry in 1977. But his lead had been halved by the time Nicklaus reached the dreaded twelfth hole. His tee shot was wet, and the subsequent double bogey made the lead disappear and Watson the eventual winner.

He didn't wind up anywhere near first place in the 1982 Masters, and the 1983 edition was when Nicklaus had to withdraw because of back trouble. In the 1984 tournament, Jack had his worst bout of bad putting ever at Augusta National on the par-3 fourth hole of the first round. His tee shot landed twenty-five feet from the stick. He needed four putts from there—which had never happened to him before—to secure a double bogey. No doubt he was happy for Ben Crenshaw and the comeback his Masters victory represented, but it still grated to watch someone else slip on the green jacket. Shooting a two-under-par 70 in the final round was little consolation.

"Does it bother me any less not to play well in the majors?" Nicklaus said to Dave Anderson of the *New York Times*. "No, it bothers me a lot. I try to hide it. I don't do a very good job of it, do I?"

However, it was an occasion for Anderson to compile a summary of Jack's history at Augusta National. In his twenty-five Masters, Nicklaus had earned over three hundred thousand dollars, far more than any other player, and had finished in the top five fourteen times. Of his ninety-three rounds previous to 1984, forty-eight were under par. His average score in those ninety-three rounds was 71.23, bested only by Tom Watson's 71.16 for thirty-eight rounds.

Life was better at Augusta National in 1985, when Jack tied for sixth. But that turned out to be another year without a major. And it wasn't like they were being captured by players who could be considered true rivals of his. As James Achenbach observed in *Golfweek*: "The major championships in 1985 had been won by the stealth foursome of Bernhard Langer, Andy North, Sandy Lyle and Hubert Green. No golf icons there."

A comparison of Nicklaus's 1980 and 1985 seasons on the PGA Tour clearly indicated a golfer whose career was riding into the sunset. In 1980 Nicklaus had won twice (both of them majors), had a stroke average of 70.86, finished fourth and thirty-third in the year's other two majors, and earned $172,386. In 1985, he had no wins, a stroke average of 71.81, and had finished sixth and thirty-second in two majors and missed the cut in the other two. Nicklaus earned $165,456, which at first glance is only seven thousand dollars less than in 1980, but purses had risen considerably during those five years.

More than ever before, Nicklaus was questioning his ability and reasons to continue as a competitor on the tour. In 1985 he mused, in a Hamlet-like soliloquy, about the post-1980 seasons: "Was I playing for my personal enjoyment, or because I believed I could still win, or to give something back to the game, or to try to extend my record for others to aim at, or for some combination of all of those reasons? If so, fine—they remained my goals. What worried me was the suspicion that my continued playing was mostly an ego trip—that, after all the years of success, my psyche simply wouldn't let me stop."

For some, to see Nicklaus in the 1986 Masters was to observe a fading great going through the motions, and as a past champion he could of course continue to do so as long as he chose. The 74 on Thursday was evidence of a perfunctory effort, though the 71 in the second round showed some of the old spark.

For Jack, like the forty-seven other players who had made it to the week-end, it was all about actually moving up on moving-up day. But after the day's early holes, he still had to show improvement.

23

In the middle of the third round of the 1986 Masters, Seve Ballesteros was in the midst of a parade of pars. The birdie at 3 had been the highlight of the round, and then he got into a rut, parring every hole from 4 on. While the patrons and the press expected more out of Ballesteros, especially with such benign weather conditions that day, being able to par Amen Corner and being one under for the day after twelve holes meant that he was certainly not losing ground. A couple of good breaks on the rest of the back nine and he would be at or near the top of the leaderboard.

He would not have said such a thing to reporters after the round, but Ballesteros knew that with two green jackets already, no one of his generation of players would be more intimidating if, when Sunday's round began, he was within a stroke or two of the lead.

Greg Norman was having a very nice time in the middle of his round. The Shark birdied four of six holes during a stretch in which he appeared to be at his most confident yet was not being rash with the driver or putter. About Amen Corner, he said, "Every time you pick up strokes around there, it's a nice feather in your cap. It was probably the easiest it could play today."

He added: "I've been trying to control my ego. I was always trying to play the golf course too aggressively, and you really can't do that around here because you can't be aggressive with the speed of the greens. I've changed my line of thinking coming into this tournament."

Ben Crenshaw began to have thoughts of fitting into another Masters blazer . . . and then he ran into the tenth hole. His chip shot went past the hole, and as a consequence he suffered his first bogey since the fifteenth hole the day before. The poor chip and the missed par putt that followed, he later said, "got me going in a bad way."

To say the least. He missed putts of ten and twelve feet for birdie on 11 and 12. Another player might not have been so bothered by that, but the best part of Crenshaw's game had always been his work on the greens. If that was shaky, the afternoon could grow quite long. Perhaps he could make progress over the last six holes.

Tommy Nakajima was also having a hard time. By the time he stood on the twelfth tee, his three under had turned into even par on the day. But his calm demeanor remained. He had surpassed Isao Aoki as Japan's most successful golfer, and many of his wins had been grind-it-out affairs. He parred 12 and thought he had put the train back on the tracks.

The two Toms were enjoying their rounds as a pair. Watson was the longer hitter, and he took advantage of the benign conditions to launch his ball well down the fairways. Though not as long as Watson, Kite birdied the two par-5s on the front nine. "Tom and I kind of spurred each other on," Kite later explained. "It was a nice, relaxing day with both of us playing well."

Bernhard Langer was having a nice day too. He didn't do anything astonishing, but he was consistently chipping away at par. A couple of missed putts didn't faze him, nor did the almost surrealistic black-and-white-checkered pants he wore.

It was during the middle of the round that Jack's day turned from solid to superb. A birdie at 8 got things going. Then he birdied 9. He took a breather on 10, recording only a par. Then he birdied the first two holes of Amen Corner. For the first time in the tournament, after that birdie on 12, his name went up on the leaderboard. (In 1986, there were actually twelve leaderboards on the Augusta National course—five were sized seventeen by thirty-four feet, five were twelve by twenty-four, and two were eight by sixteen.)

Nicklaus had not played in a PGA Tour event since the second week in February, so maybe his play on those first forty-three holes, in which he hovered around par, was a way of chipping off some of the rust. Or maybe he was just having a little hot streak and par golf would take over again. His last six holes on Saturday would determine if he would be a fan favorite as a fading star or as a genuine contender.

24

Nick Price—who at the 1986 Masters was listed as South African though he had been born in Rhodesia—was grateful to still be playing at Augusta National on Saturday. On Thursday he had shot a 79, and someone who would come to be known as one of the nicest players on tour was boiling over that. His strong second-round 69 was barely enough to allow him to make the cut; he had only a stroke to spare.

The twenty-eight-year-old—who looked eighteen, especially with his puffy hedgehog haircut—had a spotty record in major championships thus far. He'd come in second in the 1982 British Open and within shouting distance of the lead in the 1985 PGA Championship, but otherwise he hadn't made much of an impression. Until his 69 on Friday, his lowest score in a Masters was 76 two years earlier, when he hadn't made the cut.

"I started the day hoping to break 70 again," he admitted to reporters after Friday's round. "I just wanted to break par and get in close to the lead, maybe get back to even par."

So teeing off on Saturday felt to Price like a bonus. He expressed his gratitude by bogeying the first hole. A part of him had to be muttering, "This is not going to be a good day at all."

But the day got better—incredibly so.

A birdie at the second hole evened out the round right away. Pars on the third and fourth holes indicated to Price that at least he could play steady golf. On the fifth hole, he launched his ball from the fairway with a 5-iron, and it landed just a dozen feet from the flag stick. He sank that putt to put him under par for the first time that day. His caddie was David McNeilly from Ireland, who had performed a sort of jig when Price birdied 2. To be on the safe side, he did it again after the ball found the cup on 5.

McNeilly would almost get tired of dancing on this day.

Price was hotter than the Augusta air. He birdied 6, sinking the putt from fifteen feet away. Price parred the next hole, then on 8 his wedge shot wound up only six feet from the stick. Another putt, another birdie. He finished the front nine with a par on the ninth hole.

He had shot a 33. It was, so far, one of the best rounds of the year for Price, and it was happening in a major. If he could duplicate that, a six-under-par 66 should put him within a few shots of the leader going into Sunday, unless Ballesteros or perhaps Langer had a similar round. In only his second Masters, Nick Price was enjoying every bit of it.

He was four under par after a fifth birdie on 10. He was having jaw-dropping results with his irons—the 6 had resulted in just a four-footer. But then he was confronted with Amen Corner. Price knew it had been the ruin of many a fine round over the years. He and McNeilly would be reasonably happy if the scoreboards still displayed a green 4 after the next three holes.

But that 4 was gone when the duo walked off the thirteenth green. It had been replaced by a green 7. Again, Price's iron play was uncanny on 11 and 13, leaving him with makeable birdie putts that he converted thanks to the complementary steadiness of his putting. His tee shot on 12 had landed on the green, though twenty feet from the hole. Not a problem.

Veteran spectators were quite impressed with Price's play. Many of them had been at Augusta National to witness Ben Hogan's Saturday masterpiece in 1967, when he had painted a 30 on the back nine. This was different, however. Price's portrait of excellence looked like it would last an entire round. And unlike the Wee Ice Mon, Price was having fun out there and was not afraid to smile. And the Hawk's caddie had never danced an Irish jig.

On 14, the former member of the Rhodesian Air Force came back to earth. Not with a bogey, though—his putt barely missed, and he had to settle for "only" a par. Still, there was a buzz throughout the course. Price was seven under with just five holes to play, and he had rocketed up the leaderboard. Forget Greg, Seve, and Bernhard—Nicky, as he was often referred to, was on track to be the leader in the clubhouse. Unless something very odd happened, Price was going to post a score that would be like throwing a gauntlet down to the rest of the field.

Part of that field was Bruce Lietzke, who was partnered with Price. He was having a very good round and would shoot a 68, but who noticed? He tried to, later saying, "I never lost touch with the fact that I was shooting a good score. It's easy to do that when you're playing with someone shooting that kind of round."

Price played 15 as though he had grown up a member of Augusta National, with a four-foot putt for birdie taking him to eight under. The size of the gallery at 15 had swollen considerably, and Price was given a big ovation. His tee shot at the par-3 sixteenth was near perfect, with the ball coming to rest three feet from the stick. The three-footer put him at nine under, a level of stratosphere no golfer had ever risen to at Augusta National in the previous forty-nine Masters Tournaments. (Ballesteros was preparing to putt on the sixth green when Price's birdie putt fell in. During the cheering, Seve turned to the crowd and shouted, "Shut up!")

Some patrons groaned at 17 when his putt missed and Price had to settle for par. And, alas, it was the same at 18 when his ball rimmed the cup and spun out. (An estimated ten thousand people were crowded around the eighteenth green.) "I didn't want to leave that putt short," Price said about his assertive stroke. "I wanted to see if I could shoot 62. I didn't want to back off. I wanted to prove something to myself." When the putt didn't drop, Price held his head for a few moments.

Still, no one, certainly not Price or his dancing caddie, was disappointed: a 63 was a remarkable achievement.

"I've caddied for Nick Faldo when he shot a 62, but this is the best round of golf I've ever seen," McNeilly said. "Believe me, Price was enjoying every step of it."

"This is the tournament every youngster dreams about when he grows up in golf," Price told reporters, adding that he was eleven or twelve when he watched his first Masters in Rhodesia. "It is exhilarating to know I broke a record that stood for so long."

Indeed, his 63 set a record, by one stroke. Lloyd Mangrum had established the old record of 64 in 1940. It was a quarter century before it was equaled by, of course, Jack Nicklaus on his way to capturing the 1965 Masters. During the next twenty years, four players carded 64s: Gary Player, Miller Barber, Maurice Bembridge, and Hale Irwin. (Oddly, the very low score did not help any of them to win the tournament.) Price had not only the new record of 63 all to himself but also the one he set for recording ten birdies in a single round. The more numbers-minded patrons also realized that because Price bogeyed the first hole and parred holes 17 and 18, he had played the other fifteen holes at ten under par, an astonishing stretch of achievement.

Up until then, the most famous 63 to be shot in a major was Johnny Miller's 63 in the 1973 U.S. Open at Oakmont. What made that a more outstanding feat, though, was that Miller did it in the final round, and he needed all of it to best Nicklaus by three strokes, Tom Weiskopf by two, and John Schlee by just one. Still, what Price did on that Saturday in 1986 was scintillating golf.

He appeared stunned himself after the round, as if he had only dreamed it. "I think I was just trying to get into the top twenty," Price said. "To set a good example for next year. To get invited back."

Of more practical import, at five under par for fifty-four holes, Price had gone from hanger-on in the tournament to strong contender for a green jacket. At the end of the day, he would find out how many steps up the leaderboard the 63 had bought him. And on Saturday night, Price would contemplate whether he had it in him to put two excellent consecutive rounds together in a major championship.

"You can't back off," he said. "I've already let two opportunities to win a major championship slip by, in the 1982 British Open and in the PGA last year. I'll try not to let this opportunity slip by. That's the key word—opportunity."

With Norman, Langer, and Ballesteros also doing well, Price's dominating round further persuaded patrons and press that once again a foreign player would take the championship. As the *Augusta Chronicle* stated in its Sunday-morning edition, "Chances are, come late this afternoon, Bernhard Langer will be putting a green coat on a foreign player, who will be the fourth such in seven years, even if Langer has to put the coat on himself, as Nicklaus did in 1966."

25

For some players, Saturday had been moving-down day. The bloom was off the azalea for Bill Kratzert. The fine weather and course conditions didn't help him as they had most of the other players. Three consecutive bogeys on the front nine had set the tone for his round. Thursday's 68 must have seemed like months ago when, at the end of his round on Saturday, he carded a 76. He had finished with a birdie and then stood on the eighteenth green staring at the fans as if to say, "Where's that been all day?"

Kratzert told reporters, "The 76 I shot could have easily been a 70. I knew going into the round that I had to shoot a 70 or 71 to be right there. In fact, a 70 would have tied me for the lead. But you can't score well if the longest putt and the only putt you make is fifteen feet."

Among the others who had breathed the air near the top of the leaderboard late on Friday, Danny Edwards shot a 72—par doesn't help when others are running by to the tune of eighteen rounds under 70 recorded—and T. C. Chen turned in a 75, diminishing his chances.

It was an especially disappointing day for a fan favorite at Augusta National, the 1984 champion Ben Crenshaw. He had begun Saturday's round with the hard-earned 142 total, and when he birdied two of the first five holes he held third place behind Ballesteros and Price. Too bad Crenshaw couldn't have turned in his card then, or even when he made the turn and was still four under for the tournament. Instead of making progress after the par at 12, the wheels came off. He had a frustrating 40 on the back nine for a 74 on the day and a strong likelihood of also-ran status on Sunday.

Some of those who had believed that Seve Ballesteros was destined to win the fiftieth Masters were beginning to waver when the third round's action ended. The top spot belonged to the Australian having his finest outing at Augusta National, Greg Norman, whose wonderfully crafted 68 gave him a 210 total.

Norman was in the majority in that twenty-seven of the forty-eight players on the course on Saturday broke par. "The golf course is as defenseless as I've ever seen it," said Tom Watson. "There was no guesswork out there today. The wind means you have a lot of guesswork. Today you felt like you could attack it. I kind of expected a score like Price's today, I really did."

Norman might have been thinking of Arnold Palmer when he played the back nine, because he charged right through it. The turning point was the place where many had played themselves out of competition. With a Palmer-like swagger, the blond Australian birdied 11, 12, and 13—the latter included a brilliant putt from off the green—and suddenly what had been an even-par and somewhat paltry effort turned into a march to first place. A birdie at 17 and a par at 18 allowed him to enter the clubhouse as the leader.

"The golf course was very benign today," Norman said. "But when the heat's on, the leaders aren't shooting a lot of birdies like Nicky Price did, so you know you've still got to respect the old girl. When the pressure's on, you still have to be careful." (One had to wonder what Clifford Roberts would have thought about the Augusta National course being referred to as "old girl.")

Norman cautioned, uncharacteristically, "You can't count your chickens before they hatch. You have to sit back and do the best you can. It's a nice feeling to be in the lead and I'm looking forward to tomorrow. I'm very confident about my chances."

With his 63, Nick Price had vaulted from a minor supporting role in the drama into a tie for second, one stroke back. As it turned out, he and Norman, who had become good friends, would be the last out of the clubhouse midafternoon on Sunday.

While Price grabbed most of the headlines, a few had to be reserved for Donnie Hammond. Instead of folding in the face of the more famous competition, he had shot a brilliant 67 to be one of four men tied for second. That two of the other men were Ballesteros and Bernhard Langer made it all the more surprising that Hammond would be one of the last players to tee off on Sunday.

"Hambone" Hammond, as he was sometimes called, had actually shot only one under par on the back nine, but the extraordinary 32 on the front nine allowed him to bask in glory and a few TV lights when he strolled off 18. He obviously was enjoying the rare media attention, because when asked on television what he thought about being the playing partner of Ballesteros on Sunday, he replied, "I might just show Seve a thing or two."

Perhaps Ballesteros could use it. He had shot a pedestrian 72, and his play was not as inspired as many observers had expected. The only advantage of what turned out to be eleven straight pars in the middle of his round was that he did not go backward. But 15 looked to be a rallying point for taking control of the tournament. On the par-5 hole, Ballesteros was on the green in two, and his first putt finished close enough to the hole that he could walk away with birdie after his next putt. On the par-5 16, his tee shot came to rest less than ten feet from the cup. Here, surely, was the opportunity to at least break 70 on the round . . . but he missed the putt.

That seemed to take the air out of his sails. Ballesteros bogeyed 17 and did the same on 18. (Watching together on a monitor in Butler Cabin, Norman and Price had gazed in bug-eyed disbelief as Ballesteros made a mess of the last two holes.) It was puzzling that the best the Spaniard could do on Saturday was a 72. Perhaps thoughts of his father, who had passed away a month earlier, intruded on his focus. As he later recalled, "Sometimes when I think back to the 1986 Masters I can't stop myself from crying silent tears. Over time I have accepted what happened, but it still hurts."

At the time, however, Ballesteros was undaunted. "I feel like I play well today, except for 17 and 18," he told reporters. "I had maybe twelve putts inside twenty feet, and I didn't make any. I was happy with the play, happy with my position. I told my brother [Vicente] that it is no good for me to have very nice weather. When the river is moving, it is better for me. Better to have a little wind for me."

"There is no accounting for the hot rounds, the cold rounds, and the mediocre rounds that golfers play," wrote Herbert Warren Wind. "This was the same man [Ballesteros] who three days before had given such a classic exhibition on the practice tee of how to hit a golf ball, the same man who had won many championships by his arresting golf down the stretch. On this third round, for some reason, he had simply lost his concentration on the last two holes. There was no knowing which Ballesteros we would see on the final round."

In contrast to the dashing Ballesteros, the less-dramatic reigning champion continued his bid to hold on to the title. Langer had continued his rebound from Thursday's round by following Friday's 68 with a 69 on Saturday. He obviously wanted to make the *Augusta Chronicle* writer's speculation come true and put the green jacket on himself. That achievement would be even more precious since Nicklaus, who'd defended his Masters title with his playoff triumph exactly twenty years earlier, remained the tournament's only consecutive champion.

"Looks like a very exciting finish," the understated Langer said about his expectations for Sunday. "You simply try to put yourself in a position to win. I had some pressure on me early. I wanted to prove that last year wasn't a fluke. I don't feel any pressure now. I don't have to prove anything."

Tommy Nakajima had hung on, his safe 71 putting him in a three-way tie for third. He had made a course correction at the turn so that he was able to collect four birdies on the back nine. His score was only one under par, but it had left him with a good chance of becoming the first Japanese player to win a major championship.

Also at 212 were Tom Kite and Tom Watson, who shared not only the same first name but also identical scores in the first three rounds: 70, 74, and then scintillating 68s on Saturday.

Many players believed that Kite was due—including Kite himself. He had finished second to Nicklaus in the 1978 British Open. Tom Kite, not Tom Watson, had won the PGA Tour money title in 1981. In the 1984 Masters, he had been the fifty-four-hole leader. Kite's stroke average was 71.7 in the Masters, and the only players better than that were Watson, Nicklaus, and Ballesteros, all of whom had green jackets. In his previous ten tournaments at Augusta National, Kite had finished in the top ten seven times, including a second-place finish. He had eight tour victories, and it was just damn time for him to break through and win a major, especially the Masters.

Kite had recorded 34 on the front nine, with two birdies and no bogeys. He saved par on 13 by swatting his ball out of Rae's Creek. He caught fire on the back nine, with three birdies in a row on 15, 16, and 17. A tantalizing 67 was denied him, though, when he bogeyed 18.

But while Watson was also where he wanted to be—in position to win after fifty-four holes—he was not very happy after his round on Saturday. Back-nine putting problems turned what could have been a 65 or 66 into the 68. To him, that was not scintillating at all.

New to the top of the leaderboard was Sandy Lyle. His 70 on Friday had allowed him to make the cut by three shots, and his 68 in the third round equaled 214 and a tie for fourth. Gary Koch had stayed in the hunt with a 71, and also ended up tied for fourth at 214. The numbers were the same for Bob Tway, Corey Pavin, and Mark McCumber. The latter had really looked like he was going to finish near the top, but bogeys on 14 and 18 tempered his round. In Pavin's case, he was steaming along, advancing on first place, but then he double-bogeyed 16 after putting his tee shot in the water.

Standing on the thirteenth tee that afternoon, Nicklaus knew that he had surely moved up the leaderboard, and shooting four under for the previous five holes gave him strong momentum. A good tee shot made his prospects for the rest of the round even brighter.

"Jack probably was playing so well because there was very little pressure on him," says Tom Watson. "On Saturday afternoon he had not been near the lead, and no one was really paying much attention to him. The people there enjoyed watching him and saluting a five-time Masters champion, but he and his son were the only ones who were thinking about getting into a position to win the next day. Jack sort of snuck up while the rest of us were paying attention to our own games."

Alas, his next shot, with a 2-iron, landed and spun back into Rae's Creek, and the result at 13 was bogey. That was aggravating because over the years it had been 12, not 13, that had given him the most trouble.

But Jack regrouped to play steady golf, with pars on 14, 15, and 16. The seventeenth hole offered a golden opportunity when his approach shot landed on the green only six feet from the cup. But the putting woes that had bedeviled him before, especially on Thursday, asserted themselves again—his ball rimmed out. A par on 18 meant that thanks to the shining middle section of the round, Nicklaus had carded a 69. It wasn't exactly Hogan's third round in 1967, and Jack was forty-six, not fifty-four, but it was still an excellent effort, and the Augusta National patrons showered him with applause.

When he walked off the eighteenth green on Saturday afternoon, Nicklaus had clawed his way to four shots out of first place—tied for fourth with Koch, Tway, Pavin, McCumber, and Lyle. However, his comeback was not the big story of the day, because of Price and the overall quality of the leaderboard going into Sunday. In the final round, Danny Edwards would be partnered with Scott Simpson, then Mark McCumber and Corey Pavin, Bob Tway and Gary Koch, Sandy Lyle and Jack Nicklaus, Tom Watson and another Tom—but this time Tommy Nakajima—Seve Ballesteros and Tom Kite, Donnie Hammond and Bernhard Langer, and Greg Norman and Nick Price.

"I'm kind of unhappy with 13 and 15," Nicklaus said. "I mean, I bogey 13 and par 15. Two birdies there and I'm five under par. A big difference. I'd be a lot happier then. But good gracious, I can't remember the last time I broke 70."

He told reporters that his only chance on Sunday was to start strong, with a string of birdies. "If I'm going to put 'em up, that's when I better put 'em up," Jack said.

26

Whatever was to happen in the fourth and final round, the 1986 Masters had already been a special one for Nicklaus because of the presence of family. Barbara, of course, was there. In only a couple more years they would mark thirty years since their first encounter, as freshmen at Ohio State University. They met the first week of the first semester and by winter were going steady. They now had five children, with Michael, age thirteen, the youngest. Yet Barbara still had managed to watch her husband play more than fifty rounds at Augusta National.

Jackie, though only twenty-four, was a steady presence as caddie. What was a very pleasant surprise for Nicklaus was that his sister, Marilyn, and his mother, Helen, were also in attendance. His mother had not seen him play at Augusta National since Jack's first appearance there in 1959. Maybe she would bring him luck. Candidly, he said about his mother, "I don't know why she was there, but she said she wanted to go back one more time, and she did."

Once more, Jack sized up the task ahead by considering how many players sat atop him on the leaderboard: "Even though the list included Seve Ballesteros, Bernhard Langer, Tom Kite and Tom Watson, there were only seven players between Norman and me. That evening, weighing how I was by now playing and putting against the number of golfers ahead of me, I felt good about my chances."

"That night, I saw no reason why Jack couldn't do it, even at forty-six years old," says Tom Watson, reflecting on the tournament twenty-four years later. "Especially at Augusta National. No reason at all. He still had the talent to do it, he had the most experience of any player about to go out there on Sunday, and at only four strokes back he sure had the chance to do it. His experience at Augusta National was very important. That always means something when playing in major championships. When you've won a tournament, you know what it takes to win it again, and in Jack's case he had already won the Masters five times."

At the time, however, Jack's rivals were not taking him seriously as a Sunday threat. Tom Kite was quoted as dismissing Nicklaus's chances to win the Masters, then added, "I don't think he can even win *any* tournament." Twenty-four years later, Kite elaborates: "Nicklaus was not really considered as a likely winner headed into Sunday's round, not only because he was well back but also because of the names he was behind. With the leaders being Norman, Ballesteros, Price, Watson, Langer, Kite, etc., he was going to have to do some amazing things to win."

They should have read the 1984 *New Yorker* essay by Herbert Warren Wind written for the fiftieth anniversary of the Masters. After recounting the Golden Bear's record in the major championships, Wind wrote: "And Nicklaus has been as all-conquering and consistent in tournaments other than the majors. A golfer who travels well, he has, for example, taken the Australian Open six times. He has won sixty-nine tournaments on the P.G.A. tour—a total approached by none of his contemporaries. He is the only golfer who has earned more than three million dollars in prize money, and this February, by finishing sixth in the Bing Crosby National Pro-Am, he passed the four-million-dollar mark—not that this concerns him much. One could go on and on, but I think that these statistics are sufficient to indicate the enormous scope of his oeuvre. One wonders if there has ever been an athlete who has accomplished more in any sport."

The Golden Bear's rivals also could have looked at recent sports history to see that 1986 had already proved to be a good year for the bear family:

on January 1, the UCLA Bruins had beaten Iowa 45–28 in the Rose Bowl, and on January 26, the Chicago Bears had won the Super Bowl, crushing the New England Patriots 46–10.

Jack was not doling out any predictions. He was even-keeled Saturday evening, focusing on looking forward. "I've played about the same every day," he said. "I'll have a better chance at making putts if it rains tonight and slows the greens slightly, but if it's easier for me it will be easier for a lot of the other fellows."

With such an illustrious leaderboard, the press and Masters patrons and the CBS announcers and production crew had to feel good about the chances of seeing a truly great Masters on Sunday.

Purely on that score, no one, not even those who fell short, were disappointed.

THE FOURTH ROUND

SUNDAY, APRIL 13

27

In his 1984 *New Yorker* piece, Herbert Warren Wind reflected on fifty years (and forty-eight tournaments) of the Masters. His musings included the following:

"Early in its career, the Masters established a reputation for thrilling finishes. Horton Smith won the first Masters when he sank a twenty-foot birdie putt on the seventeenth—the seventy-first hole of the tournament. He won again in 1936, when he holed a fifty-foot chip shot on the sixty-eighth. In between Smith's two victories, Sarazen had lit up the skies with his double eagle. The other major events have had their share of sensational finishes, but the Masters has probably had a higher ratio of tournaments in which outcomes hung in the balance until it was decided fairly late in the fourth round by the kind of melodramatic denouement that might have been co-scripted by Charles Dickens and Burt L. Standish."

Wind continued, "One possible explanation of this is the strategic verve of the last nine holes. If a contender hits a poor shot at the wrong time, his chances can be ruined then and there. Conversely, a number of these holes offer enticing birdie opportunities for the golfer who feels that fate has tapped him on the shoulder and nothing is beyond his doing."

No tournament at Augusta National would confirm the eminent golf writer's appraisal more than the Masters of 1986, when it most certainly appeared that the outcome was dictated by fate.

The weather and thus the playing conditions on Sunday were similar to the day before: no breeze to speak of, an early-afternoon temperature of 85 degrees, 50 percent humidity, and mostly sunny. The greens were a tad firmer, but because the humidity was a tad higher, well-struck putts should not be racing across the greens.

For the final round, Jack Nicklaus wore dark, checkered pants and a distinctive yellow shirt. While many players in 1986 wore loud shirts—and pants, and long sideburns, and aviator glasses—this was not typical for Jack. He had a particular reason, however. Earlier in the year Jack had withdrawn from a tournament because Barbara's mother, Helen Bash, had died. The funeral service in Columbus was conducted by the Rev. Dr. William Smith, a good friend of Jack and Barbara's who also provided the benediction every year at the Memorial Tournament. Smith's son, Craig, had liked the color yellow and had told Nicklaus more than once that it would bring him luck. The shirt he wore on Sunday was, at Barbara's suggestion, a tribute to the thirteen-year-old, who had died of cancer. "We both thought fondly of Craig and his parents as I slipped it on that Sunday morning," Nicklaus recalled.

On the first tee, Nicklaus greeted his playing partner, the Scotsman Sandy Lyle, who like several of his European contemporaries was emerging as one of the best players in the world. Predictably, when the players were introduced, the cheers were louder for Jack. His drive landed safely in the fairway—a good beginning. Though many times he had come from behind to win an event, Jack was a firm believer in setting a good tone early.

He parred Tea Olive, the par-4 first hole. A less-ambitious player would have been satisfied with that, as a bogey—or worse—could have set the final round on a path that took him out of the tournament. But Nicklaus had hoped to open with a birdie. He wanted not just a good tone but an *excellent* tone. With no idea how the leaders would do because they were teeing off behind him, he had to get off to a strong start and establish a pattern that put pressure on Ballesteros and Norman and the others before they got untracked.

On Pink Dogwood, the par-5 second hole, his drive landed in the trees on the right side of the fairway. A much younger player might have said sayonara to the round right there, but Jack's experience, especially on this golf course, calmed his nerves. The Golden Bear had never taken anything for granted at Augusta National, and here he was being led by cubs who all envisioned having his kind of career, or even just half of it. (Well, Watson was already there.) Calmly, he pitched out of the trees. His third shot landed on the green, and his birdie putt was spot on.

On 3, Flowering Peach, a short par-4, Jack had another safe par. But on the par-3 Flowering Crab Apple, he gave back the stroke he had earned on 2. He used a 2-iron off the tee, which apparently was enough club because the ball landed just short of the flagstick, but it began to dribble down the green and didn't come to rest until it was forty feet away. Jack three-putted from there—the second one was only a four-footer—for a bogey.

Being even par after four holes was not going to get it done. Jack was still even after finishing up Magnolia, the par-4 fifth hole. But hole 6, Juniper, offered a good opportunity for birdie. He used a 5-iron for this par-3, and the patrons gave a good cheer when the ball landed just four feet past the pin. They groaned, though, when he missed the putt and settled for a disappointing par.

Perhaps this day was going to be longer than Nicklaus had hoped. "You're going to have to make those putts if you're going to have a chance," he told himself. But it was already after two o' clock, and he had done nothing more in the first third of the final round than spin his wheels.

Those patrons who wanted an American to slip into a green jacket held by Bernhard Langer later that day probably pinned their hopes on Tom Watson. Though Donnie Hammond had played with guts for three days, he had never experienced major championship pressure like this before, and Tom Kite had a fine record in the Masters but no trophy. As for Watson, on the other hand, among professional golfers only Nicklaus, Walter Hagen, Ben Hogan, and Gary Player had more major championships than he did.

But Watson, partnered with Tommy Nakajima, didn't start off grabbing the round by the throat. After five holes, he had five pars. Not going backward was a plus, but like Nicklaus, Watson knew that he couldn't count on any of the foreign players on the leaderboard starting off in such a modest fashion. He began to press a bit, and bogeyed the sixth hole.

Tom Kite and Seve Ballesteros, the third-to-last group to tee off, were an odd-couple pairing. Kite was the steady workhorse on the course, friendly enough, and he probably made for a good next-door neighbor. The Spaniard was dramatic and demonstrative, his eyes blazed with ambition, and he looked especially handsome in a deep-blue shirt and black pants. To many, it would seem that Kite was at a disadvantage with such a distracting partner.

That could well be true, as Kite bogeyed the first hole, birdied the second, and bogeyed the third—so much for steady play. Also a factor for Kite was that the two men paired together on this sunny Sunday did not have a harmonious history—just the year before in the Ryder Cup, while being cheered on by the crowd in England, Ballesteros came from three down with five holes to play to halve his match with Kite, and by the end of the afternoon the Europeans were holding the cup aloft. However, on this Sunday, Ballesteros's performance contrasted with Kite's only in tenor, not outcome. In an uncharacteristically bland way, he had six pars in six holes.

To Donnie Hammond on this day, birdies were absent. Worse, bogeys were not. He was two over par after his first half-dozen holes—bogey, birdie, bogey, par, bogey, and par—and didn't appear capable of righting the ship. It didn't help to be playing with the defending champion. Many watching the championship expected it would be Langer, not the young Yank, who would mount a charge. With the round only a third over, Hammond was on the road to becoming a footnote to the 1986 Masters.

Langer made birdie on the second hole to tie for the lead, and he looked to be the player to watch—thankfully, not because of his outfit; he was much more understated today with a conservative white shirt and gray pants. No doubt he didn't want to look like a Christmas tree again if the time came to wear the green jacket.

At this point either Greg Norman or Nick Price, in the last twosome, could have raced out in front and challenged the others to catch him. Price didn't, but the Shark, his white-blond mane looking even brighter because of the deep-blue shirt he wore, made a stab at it, after a lot of scrambling. His drive off the first tee was in the trees, but he made par. He was in a bunker at 2, and made par. On 3, he was off the green but knocked the ball back up and . . . yes, made par. There were more adventures on 4 and 5. Finally, on the sixth hole, he dropped a putt from seven feet away and increased his lead to two strokes.

When the CBS television coverage began that afternoon, viewers saw two graphics of the leaders of the tournament, a total of twelve players. Langer and Norman were tied at six under after four holes. Jay Haas, Ballesteros, and Price were tied at five under. Nowhere was the name Nicklaus to be found. As far as CBS and the leaders were concerned, Jack was not even in the tournament.

28

As the history of the Masters had shown, anything could happen—especially, since 1963, if that "anything" involved Jack Nicklaus. When the final round of 1986 began, fourteen players were within four strokes of Greg Norman, but, of course, someone could also come out of the middle of the pack and steal the championship, as Nick Price and his 63 would have come close to doing if the tournament had ended after fifty-four holes.

There were some very familiar names within seven shots of the leader: Curtis Strange had shot a 68 on Saturday; 69s were carded by Fuzzy Zoeller, Payne Stewart, Roger Maltbie, and Calvin Peete; Bruce Lietzke's 68 had put him six strokes back along with Ben Crenshaw, Peter Jacobsen, Jay Haas, Wayne Levi, and Bill Kratzert; and T. C. Chen and Larry Nelson with fifty-four-hole totals of 217 couldn't be completely counted out. However, the smart money was on someone in the last five groups outlasting the others.

Nicklaus and Lyle had teed off at 1:32 P.M., and the next four groups started eight minutes apart. It was midafternoon when the chase for the Masters championship truly began.

As Jack and his oldest son, clad in a white jumpsuit, pursued what could be an impossible dream, the presence of Jack's mother and sister was, perhaps, an omen, or simply of some comfort as he did the golf equivalent of tilting against windmills. But having Barbara there meant the most. During the round, whenever he looked for her she was there, and their eyes met. In over twenty years, the only times she had not been with him for every step of the Masters were when she was too close to a due date or one of the children was ill.

Inevitably, his thoughts went to the article stuck to the refrigerator door. About the Tom McCollister piece, Jack later admitted that "this one struck a nerve. 'Finished, huh?' I said to myself. 'All washed up, am I? Well, we'll see about that.' I had never needed external stimuli to spark my competitive drive, but maybe the arrival of this one was fortuitous, perhaps even an omen. At least it was a spur."

Some of the reporters were already fashioning their ledes for the next day's newspapers and broadcasts, and many of them saw Ballesteros, Price, Norman, Langer, or maybe even Nakajima as the winner. If fate was in play, a foreigner was favored. No one would have been surprised if the green jacket again figuratively went overseas, for the fourth time since the Ballesteros barrage of Augusta National in 1980. What chance did Nicklaus have against them, really?

As Dan Jenkins put it, after naming the players listed above him from foreign countries, "Jack was so far behind, it looked as if he . . . would have to beat the League of Nations to win."

But Nicklaus was not one to think about things like that, to ruminate in the middle of a round on what might or might not happen. He was of a more practical bent, thinking about what he needed to shoot to be in the hunt at the end. "I think his goal was to shoot a 32 on the back nine, which is remarkable enough," remembers Tom Watson. "He always thought of a score he had to shoot to win and he kept that number in mind. I took it one hole at a time. Jack looked at the overall picture."

If any philosophical musings were in his mind that Sunday afternoon, they focused on how his vast experience in majors and especially at Augusta National gave him an edge, and provided much of his motivation. "To win majors—those are the big things you strive for," Jack explained. "In most players' minds, that's beyond their comprehension. That's why the majors are the toughest to win. And you're only going to play four of those a year, and each one is a very special event. If you go back as far as the game, those are the only events that you really compare golfers of yesterday with golfers of today and through any era."

What he most likely could not have predicted was that a significant change was about to occur for him: a dramatic improvement in his putting. He had struggled with it in the first two rounds, which was not a surprise because his putting had been spotty dating back to the previous year, and playing in only seven tournaments in the first three-plus months of 1986 certainly didn't help.

Complicating matters was that just that year, he had begun to use a new putter. It had a large aluminum head and was offset and center-shafted. His equipment manufacturer, MacGregor Golf, had developed it for him as part of the attempt to shut the door on putting woes. About the oversized Response ZT, even the head of research and development for MacGregor, Clay Long, said, "Up until that point it was a novelty, a goofy putter."

The results were mixed. Of course, Nicklaus made some putts, but it still seemed that he didn't make as many as he should have made, and as a result he hadn't made the cut in three of those seven 1986 tournaments. The main reason he had done as well as one over par during the first thirty-six holes of the Masters was that his driving and iron play were solid.

Unlike what Langer had done when he won the championship the year before, Nicklaus was not about to change putters in the middle of the tournament. And he didn't care that some in the press ridiculed the silly-looking large putter. The 69 on Saturday was a good indication that maybe he had finally turned the corner.

Still, what happened to his putting on Sunday was startling—to Jack, yes, to some degree, but much more so to his fellow competitors, who thought they coveted a green jacket more than Jack did. They should have known better, especially as they got into the middle of the round.

"At the Masters, it always boils down to the back nine in the final round," Dave Anderson had written in that Sunday's *New York Times*. "There, some say, is where the Masters always begins. And there, of course, is where it always ends. Even a sudden-death playoff begins at the 10th tee."

Jack had gotten more family support that morning, in addition to the presence of his wife, mother, and sister and having Jackie on the bag. Executive Sports was a company run by his friend John Montgomery, and one of its employees was Steve Nicklaus, the second of Jack and Barbara's five children. That weekend Steve was in Hattiesburg, Mississippi, because Executive Sports was involved in the Deposit Guaranty Golf Classic there (which had the misfortune of being rained out on Saturday).

Steve had phoned his father on Sunday morning to wish him luck. "Well, Pops, what's it going to take?"

Jack told him a 66 would earn him a tie for first, and a 65 would win the championship. Steve responded, "That's the number I've been thinking of. Go shoot it."

At the time, that sounded a lot easier said than done.

29

It can be said that the outcome of the 1986 Masters was really forged not at the tenth hole, as Dave Anderson had expected, but two holes earlier. However, that outcome was very different from what the patrons and press might have predicted after two duos had played the eighth hole.

After another pedestrian par at Pampas, the seventh hole, Nicklaus was still stuck at even for the final round. This would not do, certainly not against players the caliber of Ballesteros, Norman, Kite, Langer, and Watson. Jack especially needed to take advantage of the par-5s, and the eighth hole, Yellow Jasmine, offered that opportunity, even though there had not been an eagle at the hole during the entire tournament.

But his tee shot ignored the fairway and wound up in the woods. Desperate times called for desperate measures, because if he did not land his second shot on the green, he had no chance of eagle, and even a birdie wasn't a sure thing. Jack thought he could send the ball through an opening between a couple of trees and cut it so that it would curve toward the green. Jackie offered him the bag, and Jack yanked a 3-wood out of it.

"Had I been in the lead, or closer to it, I would have punched an iron shot back to the eighth fairway through about a six-foot opening between a couple of large trees about twenty feet ahead of me," Jack later explained in

Jack Nicklaus: My Story. "As things stood, I felt I had to begin putting better numbers on the board right then if I was going to get in the hunt."

But he mishit the ball, and it went to the right and through a much smaller opening between a pair of pine trees. This may have been where the fate Herbert Warren Wind referred to played a role. Nicklaus would later say that the shot "was a tremendous gamble followed by a huge piece of luck."

The ball should have struck a tree and caromed off to who knows where, with at least a double bogey the result. Instead, it landed near the green. After chipping onto the green and two-putting, Nicklaus walked off 8 still at even par for the day and feeling relieved as he headed to the ninth tee.

He later reflected in *My Most Memorable Shots in the Majors,* "If my ball had caught one of those trees, I might still be there. But sometimes when *winning* rather than placing high is what it's all about, you just have to take chances."

Tom Kite was not a long hitter, but as he typically did, he put his tee shot on 8 safely in the fairway. He then laid up on his second shot, leaving him eighty yards to the hole. His high third shot looked good . . . and looked better the closer it got to the pin. The ball bounced twice in front of the hole and rolled in. Kite's grin was almost as big as the large brown-framed glasses he wore.

Then it was Seve's turn. His second shot did not reach the green but came to rest forty yards short of it. His third shot was the opposite of Kite's— it was low and ran up to and across the green. But the result was, amazingly, the same: eagle.

Ballesteros looked like he was making his long-awaited Palmer-like charge. He was now at eight under par, leading by a stroke over Norman. Kite's eagle on 8 put him at five under for the tournament. It seemed that those three—and maybe Langer or Watson if either could get a little hot streak going—would be at each other for the championship. Unnoticed was that Nicklaus was six shots back instead of eight or nine. The bad news for Jack's supporters was that it would take some very special golf—the kind only the Nicklaus of old had played—to make up those six shots with just ten holes to play.

The ninth hole, Carolina Cherry, was a long par-4, at 460 yards. Even at forty-six, Nicklaus could outdrive most of his competitors, and that would especially help on this hole. He hit a good tee shot, and as they walked down the fairway, Jackie said, "Well, Dad, what do you think?" Jack replied, "I have to get myself in gear right now if I'm going to have any chance at all. We really need a birdie here. If we can get off this hole and through this nine under par, then we might make something happen."

His approach shot created an opportunity when the ball stopped eleven feet from the stick, on the right side. And it was also on this hole that Jack's experience, focus, and discipline were sorely tested—and his caddie was tested, too.

Jack went through his usual deliberate putting routine and was hunched over the ball, ready to putt. Suddenly, the crowd at the eighth green erupted. Jack figured, correctly, that Kite or Ballesteros had eagled. He went through his routine again. And once more the crowd erupted, even louder this time: another eagle? Now the patrons at 9 were muttering. Jack straightened up and said to them, "OK, now let's see if we can make some kind of noise here."

When the laughing and gentle clapping died down, Nicklaus went through his routine for a third time. He thought the ball would break five inches to the left. Suddenly, Jackie said quietly, "Dad, I think it's going to go slightly left to right." Jack began to reread and rethink the putt, and he saw what his son was seeing.

He struck the ball. There was no teeth-grinding over this one—it went directly to the hole with a slight left-to-right curve and in. And there was indeed plenty of noise. "I was off and running," was the way Jack later put it.

There were still plenty of unbelievers. Verne Lundquist, part of the CBS broadcast team, recalls: "After Jack birdied the ninth, Lance Barrow, who was then the associate director, said to Frank Chirkinian, the coordinating producer, 'Frank, we've got Nicklaus on tape with a birdie at nine.' And Chirkinian snarled at Lance, 'Jack Nicklaus is not part of this story.' Then, of course, after the next hole he became part of the story. We covered everything from then on, but Jack was not really part of anybody's narrative until the turn on Sunday."

Nicklaus had also said, before the round began, "On the back nine at Augusta, every hole is tough." That was what he now faced.

He used his driver on the tenth hole, the par-4 Camellia, and the ball was headed for trouble—into the trees to the right of the fairway, specifically—but it got to the gallery first and was blocked by a spectator from going any farther. Use of a 4-iron left the ball twenty-five feet from the hole. Par was the most likely outcome.

But something was very different about Nicklaus now—he had complete confidence in his putting. That hadn't been the case for almost three and a half rounds at Augusta National, or the first third of 1986, for that matter. But as he bent over this birdie putt, he felt quite comfortable, and the twenty-five feet looked like two feet to him. He moved the putter, contact was made, the ball rolled across the green, and it was swallowed by the cup.

But now Amen Corner loomed. For Nicklaus, the eleventh hole, the long par-4 White Dogwood, was the sixty-fifth of the tournament, and it was getting into the late afternoon of the last day. He was confronted by the necessity of hitting as long—and, of course, as accurate—a drive as he could so that a shorter second shot had a better chance of landing on the green than in the pond directly in front of it.

That was what Jack did. The following 8-iron shot resulted in his ball coming to rest twenty-five feet past the stick. He and Jackie carefully read the green, then Jack went into the familiar crouch. While his routine was still deliberate, there was no hesitancy in it. The ball rolled across the green, and Jackie jumped in the air as it dropped into the cup. As close as he was, there was no way Jack could hear it rattle above the cheers. They were the loudest of the day thus far.

"I've never known such noise on a golf course as I heard that day," recalled Dave Musgrove, Sandy Lyle's caddie, who had been on the bag when Lyle won the British Open the year before and for Ballesteros when he won it in 1979. "When Nicklaus birdied the 11th, I could hardly hear, it was so noisy."

Covering the Masters for Newsday, Jeff Williams wrote that "Amen Corner became Yeahmen Corner, the cheers both exhilarating the players and distracting them, as great strokes were played and important putts were holed. The loudest of the explosions were produced, as always, by Nicklaus."

One down, two to go at Amen Corner. But the first one was that hole again, the twelfth. Nicklaus had a long and often unhappy history with the par-3 Golden Bell. Before the round, he had been asked about the hole and how much it might figure into the championship. He refused to answer. Instead, he said, "I don't want to be standing over a shot and thinking that I've said this was the toughest shot on the back nine."

"At the twelfth hole, there's no room for error," Tom Watson says. "There's no way to bail out on that hole. It's an innocent little hole until you've got to play it, especially in the final round."

Walking toward the tee, Jack was now three under in the round and had surged to five under for the tournament. If Norman, Price, Kite, Watson, or Ballesteros were not having similar success on the front nine, Nicklaus had closed the gap. But as he had once said about Golden Bell, "Sometimes I get there, and my hands just shake."

It sure was a good reason for the quivers to be teeing off at the tricky par-3 while on a roll in the final round of the Masters—do well, and the leaders have to start shaking; mess up, and it's wait until next year. The bigger problem for Nicklaus compared to others in contention was that he would be forty-seven next year and, presumably, even more of a long shot to win.

It took the strength of his mind to push away thoughts of how 12 had derailed him in 1981, giving Watson the chance to wear the green jacket. And he couldn't allow for the self-doubt that three birdies in a row would be asking for too much. So he simply took a 7-iron from Jackie, set up, and swung.

"He would be content with a par," Herbert Warren Wind would write in the *New Yorker* about Nicklaus's shot. "He hit the ball a shade too hard, though, and it finished in the fringe just over and slightly below the green. Instead of two-putting for par, he would have to get down in a chip and putt."

The ball didn't land on the green. With aggravating timing, just as Jack swung there had been a gust of wind. The ball came to rest in the fringe left of the green. He chipped from there, and when the ball hit the green, it hung up on a small ridge when it should have rolled toward the flag. This meant a downhill putt, a seven-footer that looked as easy as a seventy-footer.

Jack went through his routine. This time no cheers interrupted him, but he noted just as he moved the putter that about a foot in front of his ball was a spike mark. (Spiked shoes were still commonly worn in PGA Tour events in 1986.) Was this fate exacting revenge? It appeared so when Jack's putt was sent ever-so-slightly off line by the spike mark and the ball caressed the lip of the cup without dropping in.

Bogey. Once again, the hole had been very unkind to the Golden Bear.

The less-polite fans in the huge crowd that Sunday afternoon thought much the same thing: *He's blown it.* Others, even those with a flicker of hope remaining, were suddenly on the brink of conceding their hero's defeat after what had been four holes full of hope.

"To be candid," Wind wrote, "at this stage of the tournament I didn't think that he had a chance to win it. I was simply delighted to see him playing first-class golf again."

He and Jackie had to regroup. Only six holes were left, with absolutely no margin for error. Even shooting par the rest of the round would likely result in calls of "Nice try, Jack!" as he walked up the eighteenth fairway.

Jack Nicklaus was never one to think that trying hard was enough. Only winning a golf tournament, especially a major, mattered. So as he walked off the twelfth green, according to *Jack Nicklaus: My Story*, he told himself, "Come on, Jack, don't do what you did yesterday after you birdied 12 and became defensive. The only way you're going to win this thing at this stage is by being aggressive. Go for it, fella."

As Pat Summerall, in the prestigious position of being in the booth at the eighteenth hole for CBS, recalls today, "I think everybody thought, at that point, that he was going to collapse on the back nine, and the bogey at 12 was the beginning of it. He was going to have a tough time on the back nine because of his age, meaning he couldn't possibly have the kind of success there he'd had before. Well, he didn't. But not in the way everyone thought."

The players in the three groups behind Nicklaus and Lyle had noted the posting of Jack's three straight birdies on the leaderboard, but they were more puzzled than worried. The bogey at 12 meant things were going back to "normal"—Jack had made the best short run he could at his age, showing a Golden Bear spark in what had otherwise been a shadowy year. But one of them, not Jack, would surely decide the championship.

Two of them who probably wouldn't were Langer, who continued to struggle because the putts just wouldn't drop, and Hammond, who was also still having a hard time of it. He said later, "I was just trying to play well, make a good showing for myself. But I felt like I was out of it after four or five holes."

Nakajima was not making a move up, and his playing partner was not faring much better. Watson couldn't seem to get traction to do more than par hole after hole. He bogeyed 7, then two more pars left him at one over as he began the back nine. He began to play better, but by then the other rivals atop the leaderboard were sharpening their games too. "I got off to kind of a slow start," he later lamented.

Acknowledging Ballesteros's one-upmanship at following Kite's eagle with one of his own, the two men flashed grins at each other while waiting to tee off at 9. But that grin didn't last long for Seve. His drive landed in the woods, up against a tree. No miracles were in his bag, and he walked off the ninth green with a bogey. He was able to par 10 and 11 and keep his score at seven under par. He was even on the day, which might not be so bad since those around him were reluctant to embark on a birdie binge.

Kite had found his steady style of play just at the right time. He parred 9, then 10, and on 11 his ball landed on the green nine feet from the hole. The putt dropped for birdie. He was now at six under, one behind his playing partner.

Now, if they could only avoid what Nicklaus had done at the dangerous twelfth hole. But Kite, hitting first off the tee, duplicated Jack's shot and missed the green left. With a 7-iron, Ballesteros put his ball in the center of the green. Advantage Seve, especially after Kite punched his ball a dozen feet past the hole. The thirty-footer Ballesteros attempted almost went in, and he tapped in for an easy par. Grinding, Kite putted back toward the cup . . . and the ball dropped in for a tough par, but a par nonetheless.

Langer stumbled as the round approached its midpoint. He was unable to recover adequately from a wayward tee shot at 7 and bogeyed the hole. On 8, he was denied the thrills that Kite and Ballesteros had enjoyed just ahead of him and carded another bogey. The West German was going in the wrong direction and couldn't stop it.

Hammond was punchy after getting beaten up on the early holes. He bogeyed the seventh hole and then the eighth for his fifth bogey of the day to go with just one birdie. He parred 9 but didn't feel much relief from that. "Four over after nine holes," Hammond reflected later. "Things were falling apart on me. The final round just had a different feel. I was tentative. It was the fourth round of the Masters, and I was in second place." Alas, he had said au revoir to second for good.

Price couldn't find the magic of Saturday. That wasn't necessarily a bad thing, because from his position as Sunday's round began he didn't need another 63 to win the Masters. But he couldn't put birdies together to break from the pack. The putts that had been so effortless the day before now teased him—a few went in, a few did not. At least if he could keep pace with his playing partner and Ballesteros didn't go crazy on the back nine, Price still had a good chance at the championship.

Norman was keeping his cool, and, as he'd said, keeping his ego in check. Somehow, despite all the scrambling, he had managed a one under par on the front nine. As he stood on the tenth tee, being tied with Ballesteros at seven under at the beginning of the back nine was a pretty good position. And he and Price, neighbors in Florida, were supportive of each other hole after hole, and that had to help as the pressure escalated.

Soon after, though, Norman's position became tenuous. Bad news: his tee shot went into the trees. Good news: like an optical illusion, it popped back out onto the fairway. An omen?

Norman thought he was a pretty lucky fellow. Then he found out how fickle luck can be. His 2-iron shot went through the gallery and found a less-forgiving tree. Norman had to poke the ball out—and it jumped into a bunker. He got out but missed his bogey putt and recorded a double. To many patrons, his chances at the championship had just taken an abrupt turn south.

Not so much the Shark, though. "I think making the double bogey on 10, a few people might have thought: what the heck, let's just finish," Norman said. "I said to myself that I could still win the golf tournament."

Still, Ballesteros was looking better and better. That would make life easier for the Masters Tournament Committee, which had already measured him twice for a blazer.

30

The back nine of Augusta National "is where the tournament unfolds on Sunday," wrote Ben Crenshaw in *A Feel for the Game*. "The acoustics are such that the sounds rumble right across those pine trees until they almost seem to vibrate. If not for that beautiful expanse of land and those big trees, the sounds wouldn't carry like they do. But nothing else is anywhere close to it in golf. Players know where the sound is coming from, who is playing, and what the player made on the hole. I mean it. You know what an eagle roar sounds like and you know what a par and a birdie sound like. And the decibel level when Jack Nicklaus makes an eagle just shakes the trees."

Such noise is sometimes too much for a player during the last day of the Masters. The adrenaline spills over. He swings too hard, or he swings well enough but is so pumped up he overshoots the greens. The putts look longer and longer as a player's brain tries to contend with the commotion. Year after year in a major championship, very fine golfers hear the cheers down the stretch and their knees weaken or their hands tremble, and at exactly the wrong moment the ball slices off into the woods or bounds into a water hazard.

Such was the fate of several players who had made runs up the leaderboard earlier in the final round, or expected that they would and received a rude awakening to Augusta National's inherent difficulties instead. T. C. Chen had hoped to at least equal his second-place finish in the U.S. Open the year before and had begun the day within striking distance, but he wound up tied for twenty-third. That outcome, at least, earned him an automatic return invitation. Donnie Hammond fell from the lofty perch he had enjoyed for the first fifty-four holes, but not too far—he tied for eleventh. He and Chen were the only two of the seventeen players competing in their first Masters who would be asked to return in 1987.

Tommy Nakajima would card a 72, which would leave him five strokes out of first. Gary Koch, Fuzzy Zoeller, and Curtis Strange had 72s and never made a strong bid. Ben Crenshaw stopped his midround free fall but could still do no better than sixteenth place. Wayne Levi and Danny Edwards had to be the most disappointed, because they ballooned to 76s and quickly became mere footnotes on Sunday afternoon.

Such a fate did not await Jack Nicklaus. Instead, as much as ever before—and one could argue more so than ever before—during the last two hours of the 1986 Masters, he went toe-to-toe with the best players in the world.

"Knowing him as a friend and a person, I knew about the pride Jack had in his game, and how much he had the ability—more than anyone else—to put himself in a capsule, so to speak, and ignore what was going on around him," says Pat Summerall. "Jack knew, of course, where he stood at that particular time, and he had the ability very few of the players, even Tiger today, have to isolate themselves and put themselves in that capsule. He had the remarkable ability to block everything irrelevant out and yet know exactly what was happening."

It had not only been six years since his last victory in a major championship but four long years since he had truly threatened to win one. That had been in the U.S. Open at Pebble Beach, and Tom Watson had snatched it from him with that incredible chip shot out of the bunker at 17. Now here he was in the tournament no one had dominated as he had, a ghost of Masters past come back to life.

If he managed to snatch this title, it would be a win for the ages.

31

Herbert Warren Wind's observations about Nicklaus's disappointment at the twelfth reflected the attitude of much of the crowd that packed the galleries surrounding the tee at the thirteenth hole: Jack had made a valiant effort, but as the shadows lengthened and the sun became less brilliant on the azaleas, being at least a decade older than his rivals for the green jacket had finally caught up with him. For once, perhaps the last thing Nicklaus needed was a par-5, but that is what awaited the weary warrior.

As he stood on the tee awaiting his turn on the sixty-seventh hole of the tournament, he was as worn down as he'd been at any time during the day, but he tried not to feel it. He had to look up to meet the taller Jackie's eyes. There was nothing either could say. As much as Nicklaus loved the Masters and could reflect with pride on winning five previous green jackets, failing now could well be the lowest point of his career, because there would be no opportunities like the one he had held in his grasp as he had stalked off the eleventh green.

Nicklaus knew that his competitors would show no mercy. Norman, Ballesteros, Watson, Kite, Langer, and a few others—up ahead young Corey Pavin, playing with Mark McCumber, was making a strong run, and

McCumber was still in the hunt—were playing with a vigor that he hadn't felt since winning his last major six years ago.

But he wouldn't go down without a fight. Jack remembered a writer once saying that he had captured so many more majors than Trevino and Watson not because he had more talent than his two biggest rivals after Palmer faded but because "Jack wanted them more." He sure did. One more—this Masters championship.

The thirteenth hole at Augusta—Azalea—offered several challenges. One was the necessity of hitting the tee shot to the middle of the fairway. There was leeway on many of the other holes, but on 13 landing in the middle of the fairway with enough distance was the only way to reach the green in two, and that was what Nicklaus resolved to do.

"Jackie, the 3-wood," he murmured to his oldest son.

He smashed the ball beautifully. He sent it left and allowed for a slight fade. The flight didn't have quite the aesthetic grace of a Trevino fade, but the ball sailed gently right and landed in the middle of the fairway, as he had envisioned. It bounced three times and came to rest. Jackie nodded at him. Jack had shown his tall cub that the Golden Bear still had it.

His drive was measured at three hundred yards. But the approach shot offered another challenge. Nicklaus crunched the numbers as his group strode down the fairway, trying not to be distracted by the over fifteen hundred azaleas that lined the appropriately named hole from tee to green.

That darn tributary of the notorious Rae's Creek guarded the front of the small green. Behind the putting surface were a deep swale and four bunkers. If Nicklaus didn't land his next shot right on the green, instead of birdie he was looking at double bogey. Coming immediately after the bogey at 12, such a mishap would certainly mean a humiliating exit from contention.

He hit a 3-iron. The ball landed safely on the green, thirty feet from the pin. An eagle would be spectacular, but Jack knew not to be greedy. A good lag putt close to the hole and he'd be very happy with birdie. The ball came to a stop seven feet away. He and Jackie glanced at each other with the same thought: closer would have been better.

Nicklaus and his son studied those seven feet. They came to the same conclusion at the same moment: play for a slight left-to-right break. And be very, very careful about the speed, because here the green sloped slightly downward.

After two practice strokes, Nicklaus backed off for one last read. He bent over the ball. Two more practice strokes. He settled his feet and placed his putter firmly behind the ball. He struck. The ball rolled seven feet and dropped into the hole.

As Wind would write in his comprehensive *New Yorker* account published in the June 2 issue, "The cheers that had gone up for him from the crowd clustered near the green were so loud and intense that I thought he might have eagled the hole."

Nicklaus hadn't, but the birdie on 13 was almost as good. Ballesteros was within the Bear's grasp. As he walked with an almost jaunty step toward the fourteenth tee, mouthing "Thank you's" to ecstatic fans, Nicklaus silently allowed that maybe he had one more Masters miracle left in him—and at his age, such an improbable victory would be the best one ever.

Finally, the leaderboard was offering some support to his rising confidence. When Jack looked at the nearest scoreboard, he saw that he had passed Watson and Hammond and Langer and Nakajima. Jack was, in fact, now tied with Norman at five under par. Kite was at six under, and Ballesteros still led at seven under. The two strokes between him and the Spaniard could have felt like more considering Nicklaus had only five holes left and Ballesteros, who obviously could tolerate Masters pressure, was seventeen years younger. And he had some positive family support too, with his brother Vicente on the bag. But two strokes were two strokes, not insurmountable at all, especially for a five-time Masters champion being cheered on by an adoring crowd.

Chinese Fir was a dogleg-left par-4. It had the largest green at Augusta National. That would come in handy. The crowd held its breath as Jack hit a 3-wood off the tee and applauded when it landed nicely in the fairway. The following 6-iron shot looked right on line, but it was a little too much club, and the ball skipped through the green into the back fringe; a smaller green would have meant more trouble.

Here was a situation in which Jack's power couldn't help him. If anything, it had gotten him into this fix. The delicate chip had to be done just right, with finesse. Indirectly, Jackie was especially valuable on the four-teenth green. He had recently received chipping lessons from his father's friend and sometime rival Chi Chi Rodriguez, and in turn he had shown Jack his technique. The elder Nicklaus thought it might work here.

It did. The ball glided across the green, and Nicklaus needed only to tap in for par. On to 15. Four holes left.

"Pretty much since turning for home there had been a consciousness at the back of my mind that, whatever the other holes brought, I would have to eagle the par-five fifteenth if I was going to win this Masters," he later reported.

Jack's drive on the par-5 Firethorn was estimated by those in the broadcast booth to be three hundred yards or very close to it. This meant that for his second shot, the ball was about two hundred yards from the flagstick.

He might not have been thinking about it at that precise moment, but the most famous shot in Masters history had been the second one launched at this hole by Gene Sarazen in 1935. It had paved the way to a stunning victory. The Squire might even be watching at this very moment. Perhaps lightning could strike twice.

Jack took a 4-iron from his son and wondered aloud about the possibility of an eagle: "How far do you think a three on this hole would go here?"

"Let's see it," his son replied.

His iron shot, like the drive, was swung without fear, and the result was again what he had pictured in his mind. The crowd roared even louder—Nicklaus was on the green in two. He couldn't see the ball, but Jackie, with his higher vantage point and much-younger eyes, could: it was resting twelve feet from the stick. (Most people never knew that Nicklaus is partially color-blind, which among other effects makes it harder to distinguish red and green—over or under par—numbers on scoreboards.) But the cheers told Jack all he needed to know, and he punched the air with his fists.

Now for the third challenge: He was not near enough to the hole to consider eagle a gimme, but he had to at least push it up close enough for a reasonable birdie try. Too much of a push, however, and the ball could run right off the green and down the swale, and with it would go his opportunity to win the Masters.

Jack's excellent memory of majors past suddenly asserted itself. (Gary Player once stated that Nicklaus "has the greatest mind of any player ever in golf.") He remembered that in the first or second round of the 1975 Masters he'd had a similar putt for eagle and missed out when he had hit the ball too tentatively. *Don't make that mistake*, he thought.

"As Nicklaus later explained—unaware that he was displaying the memory of an elephant—he knew that the putt he had would break 16 inches to the right, because he had missed the same putt in the 1975 Masters," reported Wind.

Nicklaus bent over the putt, but something good happened on the thirteenth green, and the applause made Jack back off. His mind continued to calculate putts he had made on 15 over the years in Augusta National. Those memories constituted an enormous advantage over the rivals in their twenties and thirties.

Jack bent over the ball again. His head flicked back and forth, stealing glances at the white cup as though to make sure it didn't decide to move out of the hole before he could putt. He and Jackie had read approximately six inches of break, but it was more the speed he had to get absolutely right. Ten seconds passed. Then: The stroke was pure. The ball crossed the twelve feet without wavering, following exactly the line that Jack and his son had seen.

Eagle. With three holes to go, Jack was five strokes under par for the round, seven for the tournament. "Whoops," he said, grinning, "here we go." Perhaps he had tied for the lead. He didn't know that the cheers he had heard coming from the thirteenth green were for what Ballesteros had done.

The cheers Jack heard after his putt fell in easily eclipsed those from 13. The crowd exploded—clapping, shouting, jumping, hugging, some making noises they weren't aware they were making. For some if not most of the patrons who had been attending the tournaments at Augusta National for decades, it was the most raucous reaction ever to what a player had achieved.

"The Fiftieth Masters had just kicked into another dimension," wrote Stephen Goodwin. "All golf fans believe in miracles, and the thousands crowded into the vicinity of the 15th green were convinced that nothing less than a miracle was in the making. . . . The crowd was in a state between frenzy and exaltation, and it was growing every second. People were streaming toward the 15th hole from all over the course. They had come to watch a drama, but what was unfolding now hovered on the threshold of legend. That huge cheer had made the workers in the concession stands abandon their posts, and the fans who'd already started toward the exits, thinking Ballesteros had the tournament sewed up, stopped in their tracks, made an about-face, and hightailed it back toward the source of the noise."

According to *Sports Illustrated*, "As Nicklaus walked from the 15th green to the 16th tee, one had the odd feeling of being indoors at, say, an overtime Kentucky basketball game, but all the while being outdoors. That's loud. And wild. Six-figure executives were slapping high fives. Women in $400 dresses were sprinting ahead to get a vantage point. 'He's hot! He's hot! He's hot!' one man kept shrieking, perhaps about to ignite himself." James Achenbach of *Golfweek* remembered that "people went crazy. Many were talking out loud to no one in particular: 'Can you believe it? Jack is back.' Others were babbling, almost as if they had been moved by some religious spirit."

Verne Lundquist remembers, "I've never, ever heard golf fans react the way they did that Sunday. And nothing has ever come close, not even with Tiger Woods."

While not joining in the cheers, the players could not help but be distracted. "All Greg and I knew was something astonishing was happening," said Nick Price when he and Norman paused while playing 14.

"Because the Masters is played at the same course every year, and so many of the people there come year after year, even for decades, you can know what's going on at Augusta National just by the sounds the crowd makes," says Mark McCumber, who with Corey Pavin was two holes ahead of Nicklaus and Lyle. "Sandy's a great player, and he would go on to win the Masters two years later, but Corey and I knew exactly what had happened on 15. The intensity of those roars could only mean that Jack had eagled and he was back."

According to CBS producer Frank Chirkinian, "One sound told you someone had gotten an eagle, and another told you it was a birdie." He assured John Steinbreder of *Golfweek* that the commotion surrounding Nicklaus was not too much for his production team: "It was a very quiet truck. Only one voice was ever allowed to be heard there, and it was mine."

"I've never heard a roar like that," said Lyle, who was right in the midst of it on his way to composing an impressive round. "The crowd went bananas. It raised the hairs on the back of my neck."

Was all the hubbub too much for Jack's concentration? Hardly. According to Wind, "As someone once put it, Nicklaus is more relaxed surrounded by thousands of frantic fans on the last round of a hectic major competition than most people are while they're watching the telecast of the tournament in their living rooms."

Both Kite and Ballesteros had had good drives from the thirteenth tee. After hitting his, Seve blurted, "That's the one!" He was especially relieved because his drives on this hole on Friday and Saturday had both wound up in the rough. As he walked swiftly down the fairway he conducted an animated discussion with his brother. Clearly, Ballesteros was charged up and was gunning for more than birdie.

He was around two hundred yards from the flagstick, and he used a 4-iron. The ball hit the back of the green, but, as intended, instead of bounding forward it rolled backward down the slope, stopping six feet from the pin. The crowd that only seconds before had been hoping for a poorer result that would help Nicklaus now applauded with admiration. Here was the best player in the world, demonstrating why. Kite's drive had also landed on the green, but quite a bit farther away.

Kite birdied the hole, but for most of the patrons he had become an afterthought. Too bad, because in his understated way the Texan was moving toward the top of the leaderboard. As Wind put it about Kite: "A pleasant young man who has seldom played his best stuff when he has been in contention on the last round of a big tournament, he was finally doing himself justice this day."

And in his mind, Kite did not feel like he was being shunned by the patrons. "I am pretty sure the crowd was excited to see Nicklaus make his run, but I can assure you that the gallery at the Masters was pulling for everyone," says Kite today. "The walk between the fans going from a green to the next tee was at many times as loud as I have ever heard a crowd. They were pulling for great golf from all of the names that were in contention."

Ballesteros had them enthralled. He and Vicente studied the distance between the ball and the hole. Then, exhibiting nerves of steel, Seve stood over the ball, moved his putter, and kept his dark eyes riveted on the ball until it disappeared. The eagle put him at nine under par, two strokes fewer than Kite, four fewer than Norman and Nicklaus, and seemingly in complete control of the tournament.

Price could still put together some kind of hot streak, just a piece of the eighteen-hole hot streak he had enjoyed on Saturday. Tom Watson had reappeared on the radar, having carded birdies on the thirteenth and fourteenth holes to move him to five under par in the championship. And suddenly Pavin was in the mix—like Nicklaus, he had eagled the fifteenth hole and was tied with Norman at six under par.

The last handful of holes of this Masters was going to be a shoot-out. How Ballesteros played would determine if it was for first place or runner-up status.

Kite demonstrated that there is an exception to every rule when his tee shot at 14 went farther down the fairway than his partner's. He was in position to make birdie. Ballesteros played the hole without much enthusiasm, perhaps a bit winded by his exertions to earn eagle at 13. He parred the hole. Kite had a putt that wasn't too difficult from below the hole, but he left it short. Thus an opportunity to be only one stroke behind Ballesteros was squandered. The failure would haunt him.

On 15, Kite and Ballesteros could hear the crowd continuing to cheer up ahead where Nicklaus was. They were now thinking that as good as they were playing, it still might not be good enough if Jack was indeed turning back the clock. They couldn't relax for a moment—it felt like every time they glanced at a scoreboard, Nicklaus was another stroke lower.

"There was a cause and effect with Jack," says Lundquist. "On just about every hole on the back nine, there was a noise factor that was reverberating throughout, and no question it was affecting the other guys. And it was a particularly unique Nicklaus roar, so people knew who it was."

Ballesteros's tee shot on 15 landed in the fairway. Kite's did too, but not as long, and here again he was at a disadvantage. He was already two strokes behind his playing partner, and because he didn't have the length, Seve had a much better chance to birdie this hole. Kite knew his only chance was to play smart like he always did and hope the fire-breathing Ballesteros made a mistake.

After Nakajima and Watson exited the green, Kite laid up with his second shot. His strategy was to put his third on the green and putt for birdie. Ballesteros was still feeling the adrenaline rush that had allowed him to smash a 310-yard drive. He was going to put his second shot on the green and putt for eagle. If he went to eleven under with three holes to play, it wouldn't matter what Nicklaus, Kite, or anyone else did. He was 190 yards from the flagstick.

Then something quite strange occurred. Ballesteros appeared confused about which club to use, and he turned to Kite: "He asked me what I used, and I think he was surprised when I said I hit a 3-iron. I guess he expected me to hit something less, but then he started saying something in Spanish to his brother and I don't know what they did."

He took a fast, mighty swing. Experienced patrons could tell immediately something was wrong. The sound of the impact indicated the ball hadn't been struck cleanly. When Ballesteros finished his swing, his club was held only by his left hand. He stood awkwardly, watching the flight of the ball and, it would turn out, his approaching doom.

"Hard to know what happened," Ballesteros said. "I wasn't nervous. I think I tried to hit a 4-iron too easy. I should have hit a 5-iron. It's the only bad swing I had all day."

"He had an awkward lie up on a knob, but he hit his last few iron shots heavy," Kite explained. "It was a tough situation: the lie, the circumstances, what Nicklaus was doing, the noise. It was so noisy you couldn't even hear each other."

Ballesteros's ball came down fifteen feet short of the far bank of the pond guarding the green with a resounding splash. A second of stunned silence was followed by an odd combination of shouts, groans, clapping, and even cheering. The players still left on the course didn't know what to make of it. Something amazing had happened on 15—but what?

Outwardly, Ballesteros was calm and collected. He discussed his options with one of the Masters rules committee members then opted to drop the ball on the fairway, twenty yards back and left of the front of the pond. He would now be playing his fourth shot. Par was still possible but unlikely. His priority now was to not have the hole turn into his Waterloo.

Ballesteros used a wedge, and the ball landed short of the stick, but it wouldn't stop, not until it was seventeen feet past the hole. Leaking oil, he two-putted for bogey. Like the tortoise to his partner's hare, the steady Kite had indeed put his third shot on the green and sank the putt for birdie.

"Frankly, it scored a TKO over Ballesteros," Dan Jenkins reported, even though Ballesteros was tied with Kite for the lead. "He had looked indestructible. But the roar greeting Jack's shot at 16 must have got to the Spaniard. Seve jerked the worst-looking 4-iron imaginable at the 15th and put the ball into the front pond with a one-handed finish. He suffered the disastrous bogey that destroyed his confidence beyond repair. Make no mistake. Jack Nicklaus knocked that club out of Seve's hand."

What had been unthinkable on Thursday morning as Gene Sarazen and Sam Snead prepared for the ceremonial tee shots was now a reality up on the scoreboard: Ballesteros, Kite, and Nicklaus were tied for first at eight under. Was there enough left in the tank for Jack to hang on?

32

No one knew whether the Olden Bear could pull together a miracle, but reporters were grateful that they already had a feel-good story to tell their editors about: Larry Mize, the twenty-seven-year-old native of Augusta and an Augusta Prep graduate, not only shot in the 60s in the Masters for the first time on Sunday, but he carded a bogey-free 65. Mize's mesmerizing round gave him a 286, two under par—not close enough to win but placing him in the top twenty-four to be invited back home next April.

"It made the week a little bit better," Mize said about his round. "It's nice to finish the tournament with a 65 and get back in the red for the week." But he couldn't linger in the locker room telling tales about his excellent round—his wife, at home in Columbus, Georgia, was expecting their first child any day.

By late Sunday afternoon, though, a native son's heroics interested very few patrons and members of the press. As Nicklaus's bid for the green jacket intensified, more compelling angles began to emerge. One was "us against them": the United States versus the foreign players.

"If you want to get golf on the front pages again and you don't have a Francis Ouimet, a Bobby Jones, or a Ben Hogan handy," Dan Jenkins wrote, "you send an aging Jack Nicklaus out in the last round of the 1986 Masters and tell him to kill more foreigners than a general named Eisenhower. That'll do it." (Again overlooked was the very American Tom Kite.)

According to Al Ludwick, an *Augusta Chronicle* columnist, "It would have made a great Saturday morning movie fare back when I was a kid, Jack Nicklaus galloping out of the pines of Augusta to save the Masters from the foreign threat. It was the cavalry arriving at the last moment—make that the last nine—to save the day, the old gunfighter taking his Colts out of the bottom bureau drawer to save the town or the sheriff heading off the bad guys at the pass."

A second prominent angle was, of course, the transformation of Jack Nicklaus from rocking-chair candidate to once more being the man to beat—or at least to fear down the stretch. As *Sports Illustrated* would put it, "Maybe Nicklaus had drawn up a contract with Lucifer for one last major, for that slippery 20th that had eluded him since 1980, for a sixth green blazer. In exchange, Nicklaus would do pro-ams in Hades the rest of his days. What else could explain it? How else to explain the guy in 160th place on the money list, just one spot behind Dan Halldorson?"

The magazine went even further by pointing out that Nicklaus had played in twenty-eight Masters, two more than Corey Pavin had lived years, and that when Nicklaus won his first Masters in 1963, Greg Norman was eight years old and Ballesteros and Langer were five.

One other angle was that by the time Ballesteros and Kite walked off the fifteenth green, only four players remained who had a very good chance of winning the championship: those two, Nicklaus, of course—and Greg Norman.

The Australian's career is often found wanting by golf writers and some fans who cite his collapse in the 1996 Masters (which allowed Nick Faldo to win his third green jacket) and runner-up finishes in other majors. Not given as much weight are his 331 weeks as the number one player in the world, his status as one of the top earners ever, and his two British Open championships. With the exception of those two victories in majors, the back nine of the 1986 Masters was arguably his finest hour.

Prior to that, Norman's best finish in a Masters was his first one, in 1981, and he had never completed seventy-two holes in less than a 288, which is exactly par. When he double-bogeyed to begin the back nine, many on hand at Augusta National believed that he had knocked himself out of the running. With Nick Price not mounting any kind of charge, few people were paying attention to the last group on the course.

That didn't change after Norman missed a makeable birdie putt on 13. He was running out of holes and was four back from Ballesteros before the latter had his problems on 15. Norman heard the loud, odd noise up ahead.

"I heard a big roar and thought Seve had made another eagle," Norman said. "Everybody was following Jack and Seve and there were about seventy people watching us. I looked over at Nick and said, 'Let's just wake these people up and let them know we're still here.'"

He did, more than Price. Norman birdied 14. On 15, shots with his driver and 6-iron had him on the green. Two putts later, he had another birdie. He used a 6-iron off the tee at 16, and his ball came to rest two feet from the cup. It had barely missed being an ace, and Norman had to "settle" for a birdie. He walked off the green eight under par.

It was a Palmer-like string of holes. Norman was playing up to his potential at exactly the right time. The Shark was hunting down the Bear.

Watson, Nakajima, Hammond, Price, Pavin, and even the defending champion, Langer, were pretty much done for as Nicklaus played his last three holes. Only he or one of the three men right behind him—Norman, Ballesteros, and Kite—would win the 1986 Masters.

No matter who won, it would be memorable. Some of the players there at Augusta National knew that they were part of an historic event. Recalls Mark McCumber, "Emotionally, it might have been the most—without winning myself—the most I've felt goose bumps and that incredible feeling when you're in a situation when you know you're around something very special happening."

33

Three holes to go. Jack Nicklaus had a lot of memories of all the times he had come to Redbud, the par-3 sixteenth hole at Augusta National, with the championship hanging in the balance.

"One of the hazards of being late in the lineup is that a lot of the good storytelling has been told," recalled Jim Nantz, who today anchors the CBS coverage but in 1986 was covering the sixteenth hole in his first Masters. "You just want to make sure you have something fresh to say. When Jack knocked it in there hole-high at 15 and had an eagle bid, I was starting to connect the dots. He was going to come to 16, and this was going to be bigger than life. As he was standing on the tee, I really had a hard time getting my mouth to move. And my teeth were chattering. That's the most nervous I have been in my life."

His tee shot was almost perfect. The ball landed, gamboled around the green a bit, then stopped four feet from the pin. The crowd roared as though it were witnessing a prizefight and the old champ, who had spent time on the ropes, had come back to floor the challenger. There had to be people in the crowd who had watched the birdie on 16 that had earned Nicklaus his first championship here in 1963 and the forty-footer in 1975 that had earned him his last one.

As Jack prepared his birdie attempt, Tom Watson looked over from the fifteenth green. He had put himself in a pretty good position for eagle, as Nicklaus had done just a few minutes before. If he sank the twenty-footer, he would go from four to two strokes behind. With his experience and nerves, Watson would take that with three holes to play in any major.

The problem he faced, though, was that this was not just any major—it was the Masters, and the five-time champion on the next green was about to attempt a putt that could tie him for the lead. If Nicklaus made it—and the fifteenth green was close enough for Watson to see that he had a very good chance—the crowd would go nuts again. His choices were either to wait for Nicklaus's fans to settle, or perhaps by sinking his own putt for eagle first, to create a big roar and maybe rattle Jack.

Watson chose the latter option. But that meant lining up and putting right away, which he did. Watson's putt missed the hole by enough of a distance that only his nerves allowed him to make the comeback for a birdie.

Every player still left on the course had to contend with that extra opponent: the crowd supporting Nicklaus. "We literally got into what I call 'roar-watching,'" says McCumber. "Every shot Corey and I hit, we had to play around the timing of the roars."

Moments after Watson putted, Jack's ball dropped in. Nantz and other CBS commentators could barely be heard above the crowd's earsplitting reaction. Some were transfixed as they yelled, as if only their mouths could move.

"When he made his putt for birdie," Nantz said, "the only thing I could think to say was 'The Bear has come out of hibernation!'"

Some patrons immediately made a dash for 17 to witness what appeared to be the continuing unfolding of a miracle. Jack smiled at his son. There was nothing he could think to say, and he was afraid that if he tried he would become choked up.

In an astonishing display of power, skill, and experience, Nicklaus had played the previous eight holes birdie-birdie-birdie-bogey-birdie-par-eagle-birdie. Through sixteen holes, he was six under, and eight under for the tournament. He was tied for first, with Kite and Ballesteros. Everything, now, rested on 17 and 18.

Finally, remembers Verne Lundquist, the CBS announcer could see for himself what all the noise was about. Though not a Masters rookie, he was covering the seventeenth hole for the network for the first time. "For two hours I listened to the building waves of applause and roars that followed Jack," he recalls. "I was in the tower behind the seventeenth hole, and I would take my headset off on occasion as he played his way to me, and I would hear those sounds."

Above the din, Jack said to his son as they walked to the next tee, "Hey, I haven't had this much fun in six years."

Nicklaus faced a very unusual opponent as he stood on the tee at 17—tears. The reaction of the crowd at the fifteenth and sixteenth greens, which he later described as "deafening," had packed an emotional wallop. For sure, it was a show of affection and support unlike anything he had heard since the U.S. Open six years earlier. Jack had journeyed very far from his first years as a professional, including those early Masters championships, when he was far from being a fan favorite. Now, on this Sunday, there wasn't a more popular athlete in the world.

However, after he gathered himself and launched his tee shot on 17, the par-4 Nandina, some patrons worried that the incredible string of golf was coming to an end at the worst possible time. Jack's plan was to draw the ball to the left side of the fairway to give him the best angle to the flagstick, which could be found in the back right of the green. But his drive went farther left than he wanted, and the ball wound up between two pine trees, on hard ground.

Jack had 120 yards left. His first thought: 9-iron. But he saw an overhanging tree branch in the way, which meant he had to keep the ball low. Adding to that challenge was that the seventeenth green was one of the firmest on the course, and he had to make sure he spun the ball enough that it stopped on the green. The only solution he could devise was a low pitching-wedge hit with cut spin. He positioned the ball two inches farther back in his stance than normal to try to put a lid on the height of the shot.

He swung. The ball streaked under the tree branch, missing it by less than two feet. The ball hit the green. Would it stop? At first, no . . . then the heavy spin cut in. The ball stopped eleven feet from the hole, left and slightly below it. Longtime observers, many of them yelling themselves hoarse, recognized that they had most likely just witnessed the finest shot on 17 under intense pressure in Masters history.

Not a single person watching the Masters did not realize that those eleven feet were the distance to a birdie—and Jack's outright lead of the championship. He and Jackie read the green with extra care. True, if he managed only par he could still try to gain another stroke at 18, but Nicklaus was too much in the zone to allow anything to slip away. But he couldn't read it; the green was enigmatic, almost deliberately secretive.

After looking at Jackie, he made his decision: just hit it at the hole with what he thought would be the right speed, and hope for the best. Sometimes even the greatest golfer ever has to rely on hope. And on his experience, too, which told him there would not be much break.

His somewhat ungainly putter tapped the ball. As it traveled it shivered to the left. Then it shivered to the right. Before it could attempt another direction, the ground under it was empty, and it fell into the cup.

"When it was about a foot away, I said, 'Maybe,'" says Lundquist. "And then I said, 'Yes, sir!' It was the first time I had ever said that on the air, and Peter Kostis told me years later that Ben Wright had said the same thing earlier that day, from the fifteenth. So I guess it just slipped into my subconscious."

Jack had known it was in when the ball was still three feet from the cup. A huge smile opened his face, he lunged forward, his tongue curled at the front of his mouth as if he had just caught sight of a huge steak, and he raised his putter in the air like a sword to lead true believers into battle. Jackie jumped, and only his body, not his heart, would come back to earth.

Even the most cynical patron at Augusta National was stunned: Jack Nicklaus, at forty-six, was not only hanging around late on a Sunday afternoon but was leading the best golfers in the world.

Sandy Lyle could have been wearing a clown outfit and still gone unnoticed as he made his way to Holly, the par-4 eighteenth hole. Security members tried to carve a path for Nicklaus through adoring patrons who wanted to pat his back, shake his hand, even just touch the sleeve of his yellow shirt. If what they were seeing was supernatural, maybe a little bit would rub off on them.

The members of the Masters Tournament Committee never actually admitted it, but the bunkers on the left side of the eighteenth fairway had been installed to capture extra-long tee shots—such as those struck by Nicklaus. He knew that, though, and experience had taught him the best way to play this hole. He used a 3-wood off the tee. His ball landed safely in the fairway, leaving him 180 yards. He and his son Steve had talked about shooting a 65 that morning. A birdie here and he would do what only one other player had ever done in the Masters, which was card a 64 in the final round to win, as Gary Player had done in 1978.

Now he had to make the last crucial decision of the round—go for birdie or par. It was Jack's aggressiveness on the last five holes that had put him in the lead. The big difference now, though, was that for the first time he *had* the lead. Being overly aggressive here could put him back into a tie or worse, with no holes left to play. Jack had won plenty of tournaments with his physical strength, but as he got older he had won more with his brain. The smart move was to post the 65 and challenge anyone in the field to catch him.

"You've had an incredible run to get where you are, so don't screw it up now by trying to cap yourself with a birdie at 18," he told himself. "Just go ahead and play the hole intelligently. If you make birdie, great, but par will be just fine."

He took out a 5-iron. His plan was to simply land the ball on the tiered green. Even such a relatively conservative play wasn't easy considering the extraordinary circumstances. But the ball did come down on the green, albeit forty feet from the hole. Perhaps he had been too conservative—more than once he had three-putted from such a seemingly endless distance.

"I will never forget the ovation we received on our walk up to the green that day," Nicklaus later wrote. "It was deafening, stunning, unbelievable in every way. Tears kept coming to my eyes and I had to tell myself a number of times to hold back on the emotions, that I still had some golf to play . . . but it was awfully hard to do."

Before the round, Dave Anderson of the *New York Times* had put the same question to Ballesteros, Nicklaus, Watson, Gary Player, and Arnold Palmer: with the Masters at stake in the final round, what are the three most difficult shots on the back nine, and of those three, which shot is the most difficult? Palmer had the last word, and his answer was the most direct and accurate: "The putt needed to win on the 18th green. That is the shot you must make."

Once more the large-faced putter had to do its job. Forty feet—the hole had to seem like it was in neighboring South Carolina. Father and son studied the green and what they thought was the line. With such a distance and the speed required to traverse it, the wrong read could result in the ball tilting far enough off that even a par would be iffy.

The volunteers raised the QUIET signs only out of habit, because they were completely unnecessary. The patrons were still, breath held, unmoving. Summerall, Lundquist, Nantz, Ken Venturi, and the rest of the CBS broadcast team probably could not have thought of a syllable to say even if they wanted to speak. The eight-million-plus viewers were riveted to their screens and silent too, even though the loudest outburst would not have been heard in Augusta.

Jack struck the ball. Too fast? Not enough? Thirty feet left, twenty-five, twenty. It kept rolling along, like a train keeping to a tight schedule. Fifteen feet, then ten. It was heading toward the hole! A forty-foot birdie to finish the Masters? Impossible.

Not impossible, but the ball veered off slightly, losing steam, and came to rest a mere four inches from the hole. There was a moment of stunned silence, then once more on this sun-blessed afternoon, the thousands of people surrounding the green roared.

Wasting no time, Jack tapped in. What very well might have been, given the circumstances, the finest round of his career—and after he had been given up for dead as a true competitor—was over. No doubt for a few misty-eyed patrons, the man who stood on the eighteenth green that Sunday afternoon was a younger one at the height of his powers. Jack later explained, "What came over me was that my golf game got fifteen years younger in a ten-hole period."

He and Lyle shook hands. Then as he walked off the green, he embraced his son and they walked together. It was as though Jack was suddenly spent and was finally yielding to his eldest boy for help.

Jackie said to his father, his voice taut, "Watching you play today was the thrill of my life."

According to Jack, "The affection Jackie and I then showed each other seems to have become one of the sport's most indelible moments, and it will surely remain one of my most cherished memories through all of my remaining days. It was a wonderful experience to have one of the people I care most deeply about share by far the most fulfilling achievement of my career."

"I remember sitting next to Ken Venturi in the eighteenth tower, and I looked over, and he had tears running down his cheeks," says Pat Summerall. "And I looked at a reflection of myself, and I had tears running down *my* cheeks. When Jack grabbed his son and hugged him remains the most emotional moment I've had in sports."

"That Sunday at the Masters is still the greatest athletic event I've ever seen," Lundquist, who has broadcast sports from all over the world, says almost a quarter century later.

It was a great thrill for the patrons and members of the Augusta National Golf Club too. Nicklaus had shot a 65, with a 30 on the back nine as Gary Player had done in 1978. But for many, that brilliant stretch paled in comparison to what they had just seen, a display of wonderful golf by a forty-six-year-old man who seemed to have taken on the world.

"The experience was consuming for all who were there," wrote James Achenbach in *Golfweek*. "With all the noise and commotion, the ground literally felt like it was moving. It was a surreal experience. I half-expected the trees to bow down in homage to Nicklaus."

After signing his card in the scorer's tent, Jack went to Jones Cabin by the tenth tee to watch if anyone could catch him.

Ballesteros showed his mettle by recovering from the bogey at 15 to par 16. To his credit, it was not an easy par. As Thomas Stinson of the *Atlanta Journal-Constitution* reported: "If Seve Ballesteros felt as if his feet were slipping out from under him, that's because they were. Perched on the edge of a sand trap—and the edge of his own demise—beside the 16th green, Ballesteros could hardly stand, his one shoe two feet below the other and slipping deeper in the sand. He had knocked his tee shot onto the very brim of the trap. The more he tried to dig in, the farther his foot moved down toward the blue pond."

Ballesteros appeared to recover with a fine tee shot on 17, especially when he put his second shot on the green. He was left with a long putt for birdie, but he had sunk longer ones, and the worst-case scenario was to record a par and hitch his pants up for a birdie try on 18. Nicklaus was done; his score couldn't get any lower. Kite? Well, he had come up short in majors before, including here, so one more time can happen. Norman? Same thing. He'd had the U.S. Open in his hands two years earlier, then got crushed in the playoff by Fuzzy Zoeller. Ballesteros had four major championships already. This was the perfect time to secure a fifth.

And a very bad time for a very bad putt. His ball skidded past the hole, and his odd reaction was to wave derisively at it, as though the ball or fate and not he were at fault. He made an indifferent attempt at saving par, and failed. Right before the crowd's eyes, Ballesteros was having a meltdown. He was, incredibly, throwing the tournament away. He did make the bogey putt and then walked toward the eighteenth tee.

Then there was another odd scene: as the crowd applauded Ballesteros, he smiled and blew kisses to them. It was as though he was acknowledging that the outcome of this Masters had been preordained, and he had played his part in it faithfully. Now, for him, it was over. Accepting his fate, he told reporters, "When you win, it's great. When you lose, you have to be a good sport."

The par at 18 made it official. Seve shot a two-under 70 and finished the tournament with a 281 total, seven under par, two strokes behind Nicklaus. For Jack, watching in Jones Cabin, it was one down, two to go.

Kite had also parred 16. It had still seemed then that keeping pace with Ballesteros might be enough. But Nicklaus going to nine under had put a spanner in that. Kite had to birdie 17. He didn't. Everything went well enough except the birdie putt didn't drop. It was like the Texan was fending off fate as well as Nicklaus and Ballesteros.

But at least with the Spaniard's bogey, Kite was one ahead of him. And Seve had looked like he simply wanted the tournament to be over. Kite's tee shot at 18 was in the fairway. His approach shot was a gutty one up onto the green. Seemingly with ice in his veins, Kite could smell the championship. Make this twelve-footer, and Tom Kite would be in a playoff with a weary Jack Nicklaus for the Masters title.

In his steady, deliberate way, he readied himself for the putt, taking two practice swings. Sunlight glinted off the lenses of his large glasses. His putter struck the ball. It was on a direct path to the hole. This would be by far the biggest birdie of his life. But the ball's pace slowed. It stopped inches from the cup. Kite fell into a squat, his hopes quashed, despite shooting a terrific 67 under intense pressure with a distracting playing partner.

"I knew it was in," Kite later said. "I made that putt. I knew where it was going, I had hit to that same exact spot seven or eight times in practice. It never went left." He added with a sigh, "It went left this time."

"After the golf that Kite had come up with on the last round, it should be pointed out that he had never played with such heart before in a major tournament, and that he will be a better player than ever in the future," wrote Herbert Warren Wind. (Kite won his only major, the U.S. Open at Pebble Beach, in 1992 at the age of forty-two.)

In the cabin, someone said, "OK, that's it, it's all over." Nicklaus quickly countered: "No, it isn't, you've still got Norman."

Greg Norman's birdie binge had made for a back nine as exciting and effective as Nicklaus's, though only a fraction of the crowd saw it. He received a bad break on 17 when his ball off the tee came to rest on a sprinkler head.

Of course, Norman had not helped his cause; that sprinkler head was near the seventh green, meaning he had gone pretty far left. Between his ball and the seventeenth green were clusters of pine trees. Here, Norman's ego couldn't be kept in check. He determined that he was not going to just punch the ball out to the fairway—he was going for the green.

He got there. It was one of the best shots of Norman's career. Using a 5-iron, he found an opening and sent his ball through the trees, past a bunker, and up onto the green. Naturally, he sank the putt for his fourth consecutive birdie. And he had tied Nicklaus. Norman shared the lead with one hole to go. As had been true of Sandy Lyle, Nick Price could have walked on his hands to the eighteenth tee and gone unnoticed. All eyes followed the Shark.

His drive was perfect. As Ken Venturi in the booth commented, "You couldn't walk the ball out there any better." For his shot to the green to set up the winning birdie putt, Norman chose a 4-iron.

Perhaps it was fate that swatted the ball aside. The Australian's ball went right, far enough that it went into the gallery. His broad shoulders sagged as though he were a punctured balloon. He later explained, "My style of play is to try to win and as soon as I can. Maybe the second shot at 18 is the only time all week when I let my ego get the better of me."

What followed was an extraordinarily poignant scene. Marshals parted the sea of patrons so that Norman could stand next to his ball and survey the task ahead of him. Though surrounded by thousands, no one could be more alone than the Shark, because no one in the crowd wanted him to chip in for birdie and win the Masters. Price swatted his ball out of a bunker onto the green and stood near it, so there was no help from his friend. Norman walked back and forth between his ball and the green. When he decided what he was going to do, he chose his club quickly and struck the ball.

His plan was to force a playoff. He chipped to the back of the green. Thirteen feet—an unlucky number—separated Norman from at least a seventy-third hole with a player who was fifteen years older and had to be drained emotionally as well as physically.

Norman carefully read the green and lined up the putt. He sent it on its way. It looked good, then it began to leak to the left. The ball never touched the hole as it slid past it. The crowd exulted, but in the moments following, Norman stood as tall as he ever had in his career. He had a difficult three-footer to tie Kite for second place, and he had to sink it in front of thousands of patrons who just wanted to rejoice. Again, he went through his routine, and he made the putt. Norman smiled and waved to the crowd as he walked off, his head held high.

When Norman missed the par putt, in Jones Cabin Jack Nicklaus, owner of a sixth green jacket, hugged his wife, and then the celebration began. "It was so cute when they finally realized Jack had won—I mean, all the security guys in there just went wild," Barbara told *Golfweek*. "And it was wonderful. They were so happy, and it just made us so happy."

With the tournament done, Jim Nantz left the tower at 16 to walk to the clubhouse. He was the only person on that portion of the course, and he trudged along in solitude. Suddenly, a cart pulled up next to him, driven by Ken Venturi. "Jimmy, jump in," he said. "How old are you?"

Nantz told him twenty-six. Venturi told him, "You may be lucky enough to one day say you have worked fifty of these, but I can promise you one thing: you'll never see a greater day than this."

34

For those who had come up short in the waning minutes, the 1986 Masters was a cause for lamentations as well as congratulations for the winner.

"When you suffer a series of setbacks like the ones I suffered in Augusta over those years, it hurts deep inside," wrote Ballesteros in his autobiography, *Seve*. "After I beat Tom Watson at St. Andrews in 1984, he never won another major tournament. But at St. Andrews Watson was beaten by me. At Augusta in 1986 I beat myself."

Ballesteros never won another Masters, and his third British Open win in 1988, at the age of thirty-one, was his fifth and last major championship.

Watson, like Nicklaus, had not won a tournament since 1984. Being a class act, however, envy of Jack was the furthest thing from his mind. "I think it's sensational," he replied to reporters' questions. "It is great. He's been struggling the last couple of years. It's just fabulous."

"Two years ago, I feel like I lost that tournament," said Tom Kite, referring to Ben Crenshaw's victory in 1984. "I was in the lead and let opportunities slip away. This tournament, Jack won. It's that simple. I did everything that I could do." The valiant Texan adds today, "I was pleased for Jack and especially for the game of golf, which won that day. But quite honestly, I was pulling for the Kite kid to win in '86."

"Jack owns this place, basically," acknowledged Greg Norman. Then, the Shark's bravado returning, he added, "One of these days I'm going to break his record of six Masters anyway." The year marked the dubious distinction of the "Norman Slam"—in all four 1986 majors the Australian was in the final pairing on Sunday because he led after fifty-four holes, but he finished first only in the British Open at Turnberry.

As Mark McCumber puts it, "Jack's greatness allowed him to pull it off when, at that age, some of the players chasing him had more ability but didn't have that same something that he has always had."

Jack had to be happy receiving his largest winner's check, $144,000, but he was indeed emotionally drained as he stood in Butler Cabin and allowed a gracious Bernhard Langer to ease him into the green jacket, a familiar size 42 regular. The two champions shook hands, then it was time for the winner to take care of other business.

First, the official presentation ceremony back out on the course. Langer, wearing his own green jacket, once more helped Jack into his. The crowd was on its feet cheering and there were shouts of "You're the greatest, Jack!" and "Go get 'em, Golden Bear!" More than a few members of the Tournament Committee sitting and standing behind Nicklaus and Langer wiped tears from their cheeks.

Jack said into the microphone, "I don't know what to say. For a guy who has won only four thousand dollars this year and probably ranks three hundredth on the money list, this is not a bad win." He was off by 140 places, but everyone knew what he meant.

When Nicklaus entered the press interview room with his family, he was confronted by at least three hundred writers, each knowing that he or she had just covered an historic sports event. Among the questions he was asked was if he had ever been cheered by a crowd so intensely. He replied that he could remember only three other times in his long career—the 1972 Open at Muirfield when he caught Tony Jacklin and Lee Trevino in the last round (though he lost anyway), the British Open at St. Andrews six years later when he came from behind to win, and the 1980 U.S. Open at Baltusrol when the crowd kept shouting, "Jack is back!"

But then Jack acknowledged that this day had to be the best of them all—to improbably be wearing the green jacket one more time, surrounded by family members, and feeling the great affection of so many fans.

During the news conference, Tom McCollister walked in. The sportswriter who had declared Nicklaus "gone, done" just one week earlier called to him, "Glad I could help, Jack." Everyone laughed, including the winner.

About the competition down the stretch, Nicklaus said, comparing this Masters to close calls in majors in 1977 and 1982, "I don't like to win a golf tournament on somebody else's mistakes. I like to win with my own clubs, but I'm tickled pink. Over the last few years, some people have done things, things I have no control over, that kept me from winning golf tournaments, like what happened at Pebble Beach. This time, a couple of guys were good to me and allowed me to win."

No one believed that. Jack had earned this championship the hard way. And no one would forget it, either. "Whatever the size of it, there hasn't been a sports event in years that sent so many Americans home from the game or away from the television set with such an afterglow," wrote Furman Bisher in the *Atlanta Journal-Constitution*. In the same article, he also confessed, "This is a story I'm not sure I can write. Athletes choke, writers choke. Jack Nicklaus has brought me to the brink of my choking point—and you can take that two ways."

As Dan Jenkins summed up the tournament, "On the final afternoon of this Masters, the 46-year-old Nicklaus's deeds were so unexpectedly colossal, dramatic, and historic, the taking of his sixth green jacket must certainly rank with the biggest golf stories ever. Up there with Ouimet beating Harry Vardon and Ted Ray in 1913. Up there with Jones completing the Grand Slam in 1930. Up there with Hogan winning the Triple Crown in 1953. What could be said? That this was a story for the ages?"

EPILOGUE

Jack Nicklaus played his last round in the Masters in 2005. He was sixty-five, and it was his forty-fifth appearance. On the Thursday of that Masters, he shot a 77, and on Friday—paired with Jay Haas, his playing partner in the third round of the 1986 event—he shot a 76. With the nine-over-par 153 total, he did not make the cut. At long last, the Golden Bear would no longer be competing at Augusta National Golf Club.

"His eyes were pretty wet when he got to the top of that hill there," said Haas about the minutes after Jack launched his last tee shot. "He got me choked up."

And certainly too his longtime fans in Augusta—or, as Clifford Roberts had insisted they be called, patrons. Many of them who were watching on that Friday in April had been there that Sunday nineteen years earlier for the most memorable Masters they had ever seen.

Jack had promised the Masters Tournament Committee to end his career at Augusta National at sixty-five, just as he planned that three months later he would end his British Open career at his other favorite course, St. Andrews. For one last time at the course where his father first competed before he was even born, Jackie caddied. He handed his father a 6-iron for his final approach shot from 158 yards. Before Jack swung, he said, "It's been nice."

Jackie replied, "Just hit it on the green and make birdie." Then he added, "I love you."

The ball landed five feet from the hole. But there would be no birdie this time, no twist of fate, just a simple par. The crowd cheered one last time, and most eyes were as wet as those of the greatest golfer ever, the owner of six green jackets, the man who had so impressed Bobby Jones by introducing a new level of golf to Augusta. Jack thanked them back, then with his son he walked to the tiny green scoring hut to turn in his card.

After his triumph in this championship in 1986, some had wondered if Nicklaus would retire. What more could he accomplish? But he told reporters, "I'm not smart enough to do that." He still enjoyed the competition. "But I'll tell you this," he said to Gordon S. White Jr. of the *New York Times*, "I think I'll probably play a little bit less because of this win. I can cut down because I proved I can still win. I proved I could win another major championship." And more than ever, golf fans wanted to see him at whatever tournaments he decided to participate in, especially as they became fewer and farther between.

He did not win another major. In the U.S. Open, British Open, and PGA Championship he made fewer and fewer cuts. In 2000 he played in his last U.S. Open, at Pebble Beach, and his last PGA Championship, at the Valhalla Golf Club in Kentucky, where Tiger Woods won his third major of the year. In the Masters, Nicklaus came back in 1987 to tie for seventh, and in 1990 and 1998, at the ages of fifty and fifty-eight, he finished sixth. The last time he made the cut at Augusta National was in 2000, and he finished tied for fifty-fourth in that tournament.

Nicklaus ended his career with twenty majors, seventy-three victories on the PGA Tour, wins in twenty-two other events, and ten victories on what is now called the Champions Tour. Most of the records he established in majors still stand, including most consecutive cuts made, thirty-nine, which was equaled by Tiger Woods.

During the rest of the first decade of the twenty-first century, Nicklaus played for business and pleasure, not for competition. He presided over expanding business ventures, including designing golf courses all over the world, increasingly in Asia and the Pacific Rim. He and Barbara could spend more time with the families of their children. Jack continues to host the Memorial, now held in early June every year at Muirfield Village in Ohio.

In April 2010, he made headlines again at Augusta National. Arnold Palmer, who became one of his dearest friends, had become an honorary starter four years earlier and had done it alone since. Nicklaus had never been one for ceremonial golf, but Palmer and the Masters Tournament Committee finally persuaded him to become the eighth honorary starter.

The scene that Thursday morning was dripping with memories. The initial honorary starters had teed off in 1963, the year Nicklaus won his first Masters. Now, Arnie was eighty and Jack was seventy. Between them they had appeared in the tournament ninety-five times and earned ten green jackets.

Palmer had the honor, and he sent his drive down the right side. No need for a mulligan—it landed safely in the fairway. Nicklaus hit a high fade, also down the right side, and, predictably, his ball came to rest several yards past Palmer's.

Jack gratefully acknowledged the roar from the crowd. For many of the patrons, they were cheering not just for his return to Augusta and for following in the tradition of the seven honorary starters before him, but for what he had done almost a quarter century before, when a golden bear of a man had made them all feel young again.

BIBLIOGRAPHY

Books

Ballesteros, Severiano. *Seve: The Official Autobiography*. London: Yellow Jersey Press, 2007.

Clavin, Tom. *Sir Walter: Walter Hagen and the Invention of Professional Golf*. New York: Simon & Schuster, 2005.

Crenshaw, Ben, with Melanie Hauser. *A Feel for the Game: To Brookline and Back*. New York: Doubleday, 2001.

Dodson, James. *Ben Hogan: An American Life*. New York: Doubleday, 2004.

Goodwin, Stephen. *The Greatest Masters*. New York: Harper & Row, 1988.

Graffis, Herb. *The PGA: The Official History of the Professional Golfers' Association of America*. New York: Thomas Y. Crowell Co., 1975.

Green, Ron, Sr. *The Masters: 101 Reasons to Love Golf's Greatest Tournament*. New York: Stewart, Tabori & Chang, 2008.

———. *Shouting at Amen Corner*. Champaign, IL: Sports Publishing, 2001.

Jenkins, Dan. *Jenkins at the Masters*. New York: Doubleday, 2009.

Langer, Bernhard, with Stuart Weir. *Bernhard Langer: My Autobiography*. London: Hodder & Stoughton, 2002.

Nicklaus, Jack. *My Most Memorable Shots in the Majors*. Trumbell, CT: Golf Digest, 1988.

Nicklaus, Jack, with Ken Bowden. *Jack Nicklaus: My Story*. New York: Simon & Schuster, 1997.

Owen, David. *The Making of the Masters*. New York: Simon & Schuster, 1999.

Palmer, Arnold, with James Dodson. *A Golfer's Life*. New York: Ballantine Books, 1999.

Roberts, Clifford. *The Story of the Augusta National Golf Club*. New York: Doubleday, 1976.

Shaw, Mark. *Jack Nicklaus: Golf's Greatest Champion*. Champaign, IL: Sports Publishing, 2002.

Sowell, David. *The Masters: A Hole-by-Hole History*. Washington, DC: Brassey's, Inc., 2003.

Sterling Publishing Co. *First Sunday in April: The Masters*. New York: Sterling Publishing Co., 2008.

Trevino, Lee, and Sam Blair. *They Call Me Super Mex*. New York: Random House, 1982.

Venturi, Ken. *Getting Up and Down: My 60 Years in Golf*. Chicago: Triumph Books, 2004.

Wade, Don. *And Then Jack Said to Arnie . . . .* Chicago: Contemporary Books, 1991.

Wind, Herbert Warren. *Following Through*. New York: Ticknor & Fields, 1985.

———. *The Story of American Golf*. New York: Knopf, 1975.

Articles

Thankfully, much of the 1986 Masters Tournament was well covered by major daily newspapers as well as sports magazines, and from them and other print sources I gleaned dozens of articles. Especially useful was material published in the *New York Times*, the *Atlanta Journal-Constitution*, the *Augusta Chronicle*, *Newsday*, *Sports Illustrated*, and *Golfweek*. For a wealth of detail—and as an example of how well one can write about golf—I urge readers to obtain a copy of *America's Gift to Golf: Herbert Warren Wind on the Masters*.

Other Sources

Masters Journal 2010
Golf.com
Nicklaus.com
CBS coverage of the 1986 Masters (rounds three and four)

INDEX

Mortgs°

Colaboratve

Sutenr

thoug

K

437.6255

awk5@kent.edu